Eye on Editing

Developing Editing Skills for Writing

Joyce S. Cain

Longman

Pearson Education, 10 Bank Street, White Plains, NY 10606

Vice president, director of publishing: Allen Ascher
Editorial director: Louisa Hellegers
Acquisitions editor: Laura Le Dréan
Senior development manager: Penny Laporte
Development editor: Stacey Hunter
Vice president, director of design and production: Rhea Banker
Executive managing editor: Linda Moser
Production manager: Ray Keating
Associate production editor: Melissa Leyva
Senior manufacturing manager: Patrice Fraccio
Manufacturing supervisor: Edie Pullman
Cover design: Pat Wosczyk
Cover art: Dennis Harms
Text design: Pat Wosczyk
Text composition: TSI Graphics
Text art: Dennis Harms

Library of Congress Cataloging-in-Publication Data

Cain, Joyce S.
    Eye on editing : developing editing skills for writing / Joyce S. Cain.
      p. cm.
    ISBN 0-201-62132-0 (alk. paper)
    1. English language—Textbooks for foreign speakers.   2. English
language—Rhetoric—Problems, exercises, etc.   3. English language—
Grammar—Problems, exercises, etc.   4. Report writing—Problems,
exercises, etc.   5. Editing—Problems, exercises, etc.   I. Title.

PE1128 .C25 2001
808´.042—dc21   2001022705

2 3 4 5 6 7 8 9 10–CRK–05 04 03 02

Contents

To the Teacher

Eye on Editing 1: Developing Editing Skills for Writing is designed to meet the needs of ESL writers who have developed an intermediate level of fluency, yet are unable to detect and correct grammatical errors in their writing. This book focuses on developing self-editing skills. The concise grammatical explanations and the variety of editing exercises will help students begin to master the process of editing their own work. *Eye on Editing 1* can stand on its own or serve as a supplement to reading, writing, and grammar classes. It can also be useful as a reference guide for students.

The main goal of *Eye on Editing 1* is to provide students with tools for grammatical analysis that are easy to understand and apply to their own writing. It also aids students in the production of accurate, meaningful, and appropriate language. To this end, the grammar explanations and rules focus on those errors that are most prevalent in the writing of intermediate level writers, although the book is an appropriate review for students at higher levels of writing proficiency as well.

Eye on Editing 1 is not intended to be a comprehensive grammar book. Grammar topics are based on an analysis of student writing errors. Because it focuses on specific problem areas, a cross-reference to three grammar books, *Fundamentals of English Grammar, Second Edition, Focus on Grammar, Intermediate, Second Edition,* and *Grammar Express* has been provided to assist those who would like further grammatical explanations.

FORMAT AND CONTENT

Eye on Editing 1 is composed of twelve chapters—eleven chapters focus on particular areas of grammar, while the final chapter provides further practice. The eleven chapters may be used in any order, and the final chapter may be drawn on as needed.

Each of the first eleven chapters is composed of four sections. Each chapter begins with a Pretest with sentence-level items that highlight the main points covered in the chapter. The Pretest allows teachers and students to assess the student's prior knowledge of the topic. The following section, Editing Focus, includes grammar explanations. When explanations are broken into subtopics, each subtopic ends with a short, sentence-level Self Check, which enables students to verify their understanding of the subtopic before moving to the next. Charts and examples are used extensively to illustrate and visually reinforce the grammar points.

The exercises in the Editing Practice section focus on the task of editing discourse—a skill students need to apply to their own writing. The exercises move students from the sentence to the discourse level, and from more guided to less guided tasks. Exercise 1, like the Pretest, asks students to locate errors in sentence-level items. Exercises 2–4 provide paragraph-level editing practice based on adapted student writing. In Exercise 2, errors are pointed out for the student to correct; Exercise 3 is generally a fill-in-the-blank exercise, which requires students to supply the correct form of the given word; Exercise 4 asks students to locate and correct grammar errors in an unmarked piece of writing. Students are always told how many errors they must identify; however, just as in their own writing, they must scrutinize all sentences in order to edit the piece successfully. The exercises are appropriate for homework, in-class practice, or quizzes.

Each chapter ends with Writing Topics—two guided writing tasks that encourage students to produce and edit for the grammatical structures presented in the chapter.

The writing topics are based on themes of current interest. These topics are designed for paragraph writing but can be used for longer essays as well.

Chapter 12 consists of paragraph-level editing exercises that are similar to Exercise 4 in the earlier chapters. However, it requires students to edit for more than one grammar point in each essay.

The first appendix, Practice with Authentic Language, contains excerpts from published writing. In this exercise, students must select the correct form from alternatives. The next four appendices offer students a reference guide to irregular verbs, spelling and punctuation, preposition use, and commonly used correction symbols. The editing log found in Appendix 6 asks students to record and correct their grammar mistakes so that they will become aware of the errors they make most frequently. The final appendix is a grammar correlation between topics presented in *Eye on Editing 1* and *Fundamentals of English Grammar, Second Edition, Focus on Grammar, Intermediate, Second Edition,* and *Grammar Express.* An answer key is also provided.

COLLABORATIVE AND ORAL ACTIVITIES

Eye on Editing 1 lends itself to individual work but is easily adapted to include more communicative activities. Suggestions for collaborative and oral activities include the following:

- After students take the Pretest, ask them to predict the grammar rules for that chapter.

- Ask pairs of students to create editing exercises based on their own writing, focusing on the target structures.

- Ask students to submit samples of a target error from their own writing for the development of more exercises.

- Use peer response for written exercises. Partners provide oral feedback on grammar topics and rhetorical issues.

- Ask students to read their original paragraphs or exercises aloud to a partner to listen for grammatical correctness.

- Ask students to read their partner's writing aloud so that the writers can hear what they have written and check for errors.

- Ask a small group of students to develop a lesson about or an explanation of one grammar topic and present it to the class.

- Have partners, small groups, or the entire class discuss the writing topics. This will help students to develop their ideas before they begin the writing assignment.

- Ask students to work collaboratively on the paragraph writing assignments, and have each small group submit its work in the form of a collective group paragraph.

- Ask pairs or small groups to look at additional pieces of published writing and find examples of the target grammatical structures.

- Have a class discussion on the rhetorical features seen in the pieces of published writing in Appendix 1.

To the Student

Eye on Editing 1 presents the rules and practice you need to become a better writer and a better editor of your writing. This book has a number of features that will help you accomplish these goals.

GRAMMAR TOPICS: The grammar topics in *Eye on Editing 1* have been chosen from samples of student writing. The errors you will focus on are ones that student writers make often and need to correct. Through practice, you will begin to find, correct, and eventually eliminate these common errors in your own writing.

BRIEF EXPLANATIONS: The brief, clear grammar explanations will help you focus on the key points. The charts and appendices provide handy tools for quick reference.

STUDENT WRITING: Most exercises are based on student writing. Therefore, the exercises reflect topics and grammar points that are relevant to student writers.

SEQUENCE OF EXERCISES: The pretests help you assess your knowledge of each grammar topic and decide how much practice you need. The subsequent exercises in each chapter become progressively more difficult, allowing you to build skills and confidence as you work through the exercises. Finally, you are given the chance to produce and edit your own writing.

EXTRA EDITING: In general, when you edit your own writing you will be looking for various types of errors, not just one type. Therefore, in Chapter 12, you will have additional practice editing for more than one error type in each exercise.

PUBLISHED WRITING: It is always helpful to notice how professional writers use the language. The Practice with Authentic Language exercises in Appendix 1 are drawn from published articles. They will allow you to become more aware of the structures used in published material.

EDITING LOG: The editing log found in Appendix 6 will help you focus on the grammar errors that you make most frequently. By recording the grammar mistakes that your teacher finds in your paragraphs and essays, you will begin to see a pattern of certain errors. Once you know your grammar weaknesses, you can successfully edit for and eliminate them in future writing.

Acknowledgments

There are a number of people who were crucial in helping develop *Eye on Editing 1* from piloting through publication. I truly appreciate the contributions of my colleagues at the University of California, Irvine. The combined experiences and expertise of Colleen Hildebrand, Susan Earle-Carlin, and Robin Scarcella were invaluable in guiding my efforts. In addition, this book would not be possible without the many students at UCI who worked through numerous drafts of each and every exercise. I would also like to thank the editors and reviewers at Pearson Education. Laura Le Dréan, Louisa Hellegers, Penny Laporte, Stacey Hunter, Melissa Leyva, and Randie Falk were knowledgeable and patient in developing the final version of *Eye on Editing 1*. Finally, I want to thank my family and my husband, Paul, whose enthusiasm for this project has pulled me through.

CHAPTER 1

Present Time Tenses

PRETEST

Check your understanding of the present tenses. Put a check (✓) next to the sentences that are correct.

____ 1. I am loving classic English novels.

____ 2. Our professor is sick since Monday.

____ 3. My grandmother likes to tell me stories about her childhood. She still has remembered so much about her youth.

____ 4. My neighbor leaves for work at 7:30 every morning.

____ 5. Right now Pat has searched for information on the Internet.

____ 6. Mary and I have seen all of the old silent films that came out of Hollywood.

____ 7. Bob and Jack usually are working out at the gym five days a week.

____ 8. Mark studies Swedish for five years.

____ 9. At the moment, I am reading the newspaper.

____ 10. I like to discuss current events, so I read the newspaper every day.

EDITING FOCUS

The three verb tenses discussed in this chapter—the simple present, present progressive, and present perfect—are all present time tenses. However, the three tenses have different uses. As writer and editor of your writing, you need to make sure that you choose the correct tense.

Simple present	He **takes** vitamins every day.
Present progressive	We **are working** on a project right now.
Present perfect	I **have driven** there many times.

SIMPLE PRESENT TENSE

FORMING THE SIMPLE PRESENT

1. Use the base (simple) form of the verb and add -s for third person singular subjects (*he, she, it, John, my aunt,* etc.).

Subject	Verb	
I / You / We / They	**run**	twice a week.
He / She / It	**runs**	twice a week.

2. The -s ending becomes -es or -ies with certain verbs.
   If the verb ends in -ch, -sh, -ss, -x, or -zz, add -es.

   watch → watches   kiss → kisses   buzz → buzzes
   crash → crashes   mix → mixes

   If the verb ends in a consonant + -y, drop the -y and add -ies. If the verb ends in a vowel + -y, just add -s.

   carry → carries   fly → flies
   BUT
   pay → pays

3. Certain verbs, including *be, have,* and *do,* are irregular in the simple present.

Subject	*Be*	
I	**am**	hungry.
He / She / It	**is**	hungry.
We / You / They	**are**	hungry.

Subject	Have	
I / You / We / They	have	a problem.
He / She / It	has	a problem.

Subject	Do	
I / You / We / They	do	the work quickly.
He/ She / It	does	the work quickly.

4. In questions and negatives, use the auxiliary verb *do* or *does* + the base form of the verb except when the verb is *be*. Notice that the auxiliary verb *do* is also used with the main verb *do*.

Do you **like** old movies?

Do you usually **do** your homework after school?

BUT
Is he a student?

I usually **don't like** old movies.

No, I often **don't do** my homework until after dinner.

He **isn't** a student anymore.

USING THE SIMPLE PRESENT

1. Use the simple present to write about habits and routines—about actions and situations that happen regularly.

I **meet** my study group weekly.

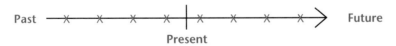

Past   ———×———×———×———×—|—×———×———×———×——⟶   Future

Present

You **travel** so much.
He usually **washes** his sweaters by hand.

2. Use the simple present to express actions and situations that are always true—for example, facts.
New Guinea **is** an island.
The Earth **revolves** around the sun. (*scientific fact*)
That road **curves** very sharply. (*always true*)

NOTE: The simple present also has a future time use. Use it to write about scheduled events. (See Chapter 4.)

3. Use the simple present with non-action verbs (also called stative verbs). Non-action verbs express thoughts, feelings, senses, possession, and appearance. Avoid using these verbs in the progressive form.

Thoughts: (dis)agree, believe, know, mean, recall, remember, think (= *believe*), understand

She **believes** you.

Feelings: appreciate, hate, (dis)like, love, need, prefer, want

I **like** chocolate ice cream more than vanilla ice cream.

Senses: feel, hear, see, smell, taste

We **hear** loud music from the apartment next door.

Possession: be, belong, have, own

I **have** three dogs at home.

Appearance: appear, be, look, seem

You **look** a little tired today.

TIP

Edit carefully with the verb *remember.* Frequently, the act of remembering is in the present and the event that you remember is in the past.

I **remember** the day we **moved** to our new house.

NOT

I remembered the day we moved to our new house.

4. Time words used with the simple present include the following:

always	usually	regularly	occasionally	rarely
normally	often	sometimes	seldom	never
on Fridays	annually	every week	monthly	daily

We *rarely* **take** the bus to school.
Mary and Kelly **go** to the movies *on Fridays*.

SELF CHECK 1

Correct the errors in verb tense.

1. My sister don't like to read.

2. Water is freezing at 32° Fahrenheit.

3. Steve is belonging to the club for economics students.

4. We have gone there all the time.

5. The director have a new computer.

PRESENT PROGRESSIVE TENSE

FORMING THE PRESENT PROGRESSIVE

Use a simple present form of the auxiliary verb *be* (*am, is, are*) + the present participle (*-ing* form) of the verb.

Subject	Verb
I	**am leaving**.
He / She / It	**is leaving**.
You / We / They	**are leaving**.

> **TIP**
>
> Use Appendix 3 or your dictionary to check the spelling of present participles.

USING THE PRESENT PROGRESSIVE

1. Use the present progressive (also called the present continuous) to write about an action or situation that is happening right now.

   John is doing his homework now.

   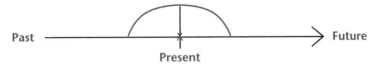

   Past ——————→ Future

   Present

   It's raining.
   They are reviewing the lab report at the moment.

2. Use the present progressive to write about an action or situation that happens over an extended time in the present. The action or situation does not have to be happening right now.

   She is working in a restaurant this summer.
   I'm studying Greek this year.
   My grandmother is paying my college tuition.

3. In both these uses, the present progressive expresses something that is temporary—that is, something with a beginning and an end. Remember to use the simple present for permanent situations and actions.

   He's speaking Spanish. (*This is what he's doing right now.*)
   He speaks Spanish. (*This is a permanent ability of his.*)

   NOTE: The present progressive also has a future time use. Use it to write about future plans. (See Chapter 4.)

4. With non-action verbs, use the simple present instead of the present progressive. (See page 3.)

> The soup **tastes** much better now.

> **NOT**
> The soup **is tasting** much better now.

> **TIP**
> A grammar book will tell you if a verb is not normally used in the progressive form. (See Appendix 7.)

5. Use the following time words with the present progressive:

now	right now	at present	today
these days	nowadays	currently	presently
this week	this year	at this time	at this moment

> It's **beginning** to snow *now*.
> They **are** *currently* **taking** an exam.

SELF CHECK 2

Correct the errors in verb tense.

1. She is knowing the correct answer to the question.

2. At this moment, Mia listens to her new CD.

3. Americans are celebrating Thanksgiving in November.

4. I take two history courses this semester.

5. Paul is drive to San Francisco today.

PRESENT PERFECT TENSE

FORMING THE PRESENT PERFECT

1. Use a simple present form of the auxiliary verb *have* (*have, has*) + the past participle (*-ed* form of the verb).

Subject	Verb	
I / You / We / They	have arrived	on time.
He / She / It	has arrived	on time.

2. Many past participles are irregular. Some of these end in *-en* (*taken, given, eaten, driven, written,* etc.). Others end in *-t* (*built, meant,* etc.). Common irregular past participles include *been, done, drunk, gone, read,* and *slept.*

> **TIP**
>
> Use Appendix 2 or your dictionary to make sure you use the correct form of the past participle.

USING THE PRESENT PERFECT

1. Use the present perfect to write about actions or situations that began in the past and continue to the present (and possibly to the future).

I have worked at the library for two years.

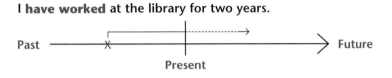

He has studied hard all week.
We haven't seen Todd in a long time.

2. Use the present perfect to write about actions or situations that happened at an unspecified time in the past. (If a time is specified, use the simple past. See Chapter 2.)

She has already seen that movie.

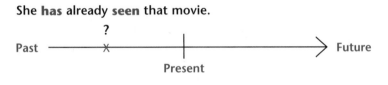

They have solved the problem.
I've already eaten dinner.

3. Use the present perfect to write about actions or situations that happened more than once at unspecified times in the past.

Maria has traveled to Cuba four times.

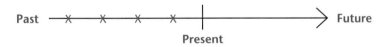

I've been sick several times this winter.
It has rained a lot this year.

4. Use *since* and *for* with the present perfect to write about something that has happened over an extended period of time. *Since* tells when the time began; *for* tells how long it has lasted.

since + point in time
Claire has lived in Chicago *since* 1999.

for + length of time
The Liberal party has been in power *for* ten years.

5. In addition to *since* and *for*, time words used with the present perfect include the following:

already   yet   recently   just   so far   until now   several/many times

Have you seen the movie *yet*?
No, I haven't seen it *yet*. / **Yes, I've** *already* **seen** it.
He's *recently* **graduated** from college.
So far **we have been** very busy.

NOTE: *Yet* is used only in questions and negative statements.

Self Check 3

Correct the errors in verb tense.

1. Robert and Alvin didn't sleep since the day before yesterday.

2. In recent years, I drive the coastal highway many times.

3. He is president for almost eight years, but soon we will have a new leader.

4. I am sick recently.

5. Mark never went to Mexico before.

> **TIP**
>
> Be aware of the grammar errors you make most often, and edit carefully for these problems. Use the editing log in Appendix 6 to keep track of your most common errors.

EDITING PRACTICE

1. *Put a check (✓) next to the sentences that use verb tenses correctly. Correct the sentences that have errors. Use the simple present, present progressive, or present perfect.*

_____ 1. The communications industry becomes more competitive recently.

__✓__ 2. The story is about forgiveness.

_____ 3. He has already went to school.

__✓__ 4. I have not live long enough to experience all that I want to experience.

__✓__ 5. My family has noticed many cultural differences between China and the United States since we arrived in 1989.

_____ 6. Her great-aunt has traveled to many different countries and still remembered important details about each of them.

__✓__ 7. The weather seems a little humid today.

_____ 8. Helen is studies chemistry now.

_____ 9. I am believing I did well on the midterm.

_____ 10. We make many friends since we moved into the dorm.

_✓_ 11. The Earth has been round.

_____ 12. I have ~~not~~ *don't* been to Canada.

2 *In the following essay, the underlined verbs are not correct. Write the correct verb form above each underlined verb. Use the simple present, present progressive, or present perfect tense.*

In many parts of the world, children leave home for the first time when they go away to college. A student's first year on a college or university campus (1) <u>was</u> often a difficult time of adjustment. From the time they are born, children (2) <u>are depending</u> on their parents or caretakers for necessities like food, clean clothing, and emotional support. After a few weeks of living on their own, first-year students realize they have to take care of these things themselves. They go through some painful changes during this transition from dependence to independence. However, independence also (3) <u>is bringing</u> new freedoms such as no curfew, fewer chores, and no siblings.

As a college freshman, I (4) <u>go through</u> these changes myself right now. Since I have moved into the dorm, I talk to my parents daily. Sometimes I still (5) <u>am wanting</u> them around. Currently, I (6) <u>try</u> to be more disciplined, but it is hard to study when many other students in my dorm are not studying. They often (7) <u>are playing</u> loud music while I am trying to study. In the past, my mother always helped me stay focused on my homework. Without her help, I (8) <u>do</u> poorly on three tests so far. Even with this setback, however, I (9) <u>am knowing</u> I will adapt to my new life, and the experience of living on my own at college will make me become a stronger person.

3 *Read the following paragraph. Complete the paragraph with the correct form of each verb given. Use the simple present, present progressive, or present perfect tense.*

One of the most important influences in life ____is____ family. People lucky
                                              1. (be)
enough to have strong family ties may have an easier time succeeding, while those with weak family ties may have to work harder for success. Everyone ___defines___ the family in a
                                                                        2. (define)
different way, and this is especially true in modern society. The family is traditionally defined as a mother, a father, and several children. Some families also include grandparents as well as aunts, uncles, and cousins. However, over the past several decades this definition ___changed___.
                                                                              3. (change)

Since the 1960s, the individual ___become___ more important, and the traditional family unit
4. (become)
___undergoed___ many changes. Nowadays, many children ___are living___ in a household with
5. (undergo)   **6. (live)**
one parent. A study of today's family ___includes___ issues such as divorce, poverty, women's
7. (include)
roles, and teenage pregnancy. Even though the family structure ___has changed___ in recent years,
8. (change)
the basic duties of a family ___have stayed___ the same for many, many years. The most important
9. (stay)
duties of a family, caring for the young and for the elderly, ___remained___ the same over the past
10. (remain)
several decades.

4 *The following essay has ten errors in the use of present time tenses. Find and correct the errors.*

In recent years, academic achievement becomes the most important sign of success in

many cultures. As a result, competition among students and among their parents has increased.

This competition becomes difficult for young people to handle. Recently, this leads to several

societal problems, including suicide. Currently, suicide increases among students in some

countries where academic pressures are high. Many students are failing due to stress, not due to

lack of knowledge or effort. However, this intense pressure is producing highly educated and

productive members of society in many parts of the world.

Since I arrived in the United States to study, I am noticing that academic success is not

important to all Americans. Although American society is productive, the emphasis on academic

success is not being as strong as it is in some other countries. This may be because this country

has many different cultures, and each culture defines success in a different way. In fact, for many

years, when selecting from applicants, American university admissions officers are considering a

student's school and community involvement in addition to grades. As a result, students are well

rounded but may be academically inferior to students in other countries. Because of this problem,

American educators now try to raise their academic standards.

All educational systems have positive and negative aspects. We just are needing to take

the good parts from systems all over the world and combines them to make one truly successful

model.

WRITING TOPICS

Choose one of the topics and write at least one paragraph. Use mostly present time tenses. After you complete your first draft, concentrate on editing your work. Keep in mind the editing practice from this chapter.

1. Most people have a certain routine that they follow in the morning as they prepare for the day. Briefly describe your routine. How long have you followed this routine? What parts of it have you sometimes done differently? Explain what this routine tells about you, your personality, and your priorities.

2. Explain why you are studying English. Be sure to include how long you have spoken or studied the language. Describe the techniques or strategies you are currently using to improve your English. Which are the most successful and why?

Go to page 88 for more practice with present time tenses.

CHAPTER 2

Past Time Tenses

PRETEST

Check your understanding of the past time tenses. Put a check (✓) next to the sentences that are correct.

____ 1. We had eaten all the food yesterday, so I need to go shopping.

____ 2. Carol took the car back to the shop because they weren't fixing the brakes.

____ 3. When I saw the tennis team, they were practicing.

____ 4. The boys bought a CD by a band they didn't hear before.

____ 5. The two thieves seemed to be sorry for their actions.

____ 6. Last summer while I had studied in Costa Rica, I walked through a rain forest for the first time.

____ 7. In class, they participated in discussions.

____ 8. I was never flying in a small airplane before last month.

____ 9. My aunt and I saw the Tower of London on our vacation last year.

____10. The day before yesterday, Tom had gone to bed earlier than usual.

EDITING FOCUS

The three verb tenses discussed in this chapter—the simple past, past progressive, and past perfect—are all past time tenses. However, the three tenses have different uses. As writer and editor of your writing, you need to make sure that you choose the correct tense.

Simple past	He **went** to the movies last night.
Past progressive	We **were living** in Indonesia in the 1990s.
Past perfect	I **had made** the plans before I talked to him.

SIMPLE PAST TENSE

FORMING THE SIMPLE PAST

1. For most verbs, add *-ed* or *-d* to the base form. This is true for all subjects (*I, you, he,* etc.)

clean → clean**ed**   look → look**ed**   wash → wash**ed**
dance → danc**ed**   live → liv**ed**   believe → believe**d**

2. Many verbs are irregular in the simple past tense.

The verb *be* has two forms, *was* and *were*.

Subject	Be	
I / He / She / It	was	in Hong Kong last year.
You / We / They	were	in Hong Kong last year.

Some other irregular verbs are:

do → **did**   come → **came**   buy → **bought**   run → **ran**
have → **had**   go → **went**   eat → **ate**   take → **took**

NOTE: All irregular verbs except *be* have the same past tense form for all subjects.

> **TIP**
>
> Use Appendix 2 or your dictionary to make sure you are using the correct form for an irregular past tense verb.

3. In questions and negatives, use the auxiliary verb *did* + the base form of the verb except when the verb is *be*.

> **Did** you **go** to the party on Friday?
> When **did** you **see** Martina?
> I **didn't take** a vacation last summer.
>
> BUT
> **Were** you happy with the results?

USING THE SIMPLE PAST

1. Use the simple past to write about completed actions and situations—actions and situations that ended in the past. The action or situation can be habitual or refer to a point in time or a period in time. It must be completed and have no connection to the present.

> I **wrote** a ten-page paper last semester.

Past ⟶ ✕ ──────────┼──────────⟶ Future
                                  Present

> They **went** to the prom last year. (*point in time*)
> We **lived** in Mexico for four years. (*period of time*)
> As a child, I **watched** a lot of TV. (*habitual*)

2. Time words used with the simple past include the following:

yesterday	the day before yesterday	last week
a few minutes ago	in 1980	in the past

> The mailman **came** to the office *yesterday*.
> They **drove** home *last week*.
> My friend **arrived** at the airport *two hours ago*.
> *In 1980,* we **traveled** to Mexico.

3. *Used to* and *would*, followed by the base form of the verb, can be used instead of the simple past for actions or situations that were habitual. *Used to* emphasizes a contrast with the present and is more common than *would*. If you are not sure which form to use, choose *used to*.

> As a child, I **used to watch/would watch** a lot of TV.
> I don't study much now, but I **used to study** a lot.

SELF CHECK 1

Correct the errors in verb tense.

1. As a child I used to watching a lot of TV. ~~was~~ watched

2. Unfortunately Richard and I didn't completed the essay yesterday, so we are still working on it. were

3. A few years ago, he gets married. got

4. When Katherine and Lee finished the test? did

5. Francoise speaks only French when she lived in Paris. spoke

PAST PROGRESSIVE TENSE

FORMING THE PAST PROGRESSIVE

Use a simple past form of *be* (*was, were*) + the present participle (*-ing*) form of the verb.

Subject	Verb	
I / He / She / It	**was sitting**	in the garden.
You / We / They	**were sitting**	in the garden.

> **TIP**
>
> Use Appendix 3 or your dictionary to check the spelling of present participles.

USING THE PAST PROGRESSIVE

1. Use the past progressive (also called the past continuous) to write about an action or situation that was in progress at a specific time in the past.

   At 10:00 last night I was studying for an exam.

   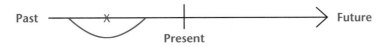

   In 1995 she was living in Washington, D.C.
   At the time the Berlin Wall fell, he was traveling in Germany.

2. Use the past progressive to write about a past action or situation that was interrupted by another past action. Express the interrupting action in the simple past. Use *while* with the past progressive or *when* with the simple past.

   ***While* I was eating dinner, the coach called.**

   OR

   I was eating dinner *when* the coach called.

3. The past progressive emphasizes that an action or situation was ongoing—in progress over a period of time—or temporary. In contrast, the simple past emphasizes completion.

> Last December, I **was failing** the course. (*I was failing at that point in time; perhaps I didn't fail the course.*)
> Last December, I **failed** the course. (*I definitely failed the course.*)

4. With non-action verbs, use the simple past instead of the past progressive. (See page 3.)

> During the test, I **knew** all the answers, but now I've forgotten them.

> **NOT**
> During the test, I was knowing all the answers.

> **TIP**
>
> A grammar book will tell you if a verb is not normally used in the progressive form. (See Appendix 7.)

5. In addition to *while* and *when,* time words that can be used with the past progressive include the following:

> as   at that time / moment   at the time   during   in the 1950s / 1990s

> *As* I **was walking** out the door, the telephone rang.
> The Beatles and The Rolling Stones **were recording** songs *in the 1960s.*

SELF CHECK 2

Correct the errors in verb tense.

1. Hugh was having many friends by the end of the semester. *[had]*

2. Ronald was take a pronunciation class, but he dropped it because he was too busy at work. *[taking]*

3. I saw my favorite professor while I ate at the new restaurant on campus. *[was eating]*

4. At 11:00 this morning, I still slept. *[was sleeping]*

5. On the second day of the semester I was joining the class. *[joined]*

PAST PERFECT TENSE

FORMING THE PAST PERFECT

1. Use the auxiliary verb *had* + the past participle (*-ed*) form of the verb.

Subject	Verb	
I / You / He / She / It / We / They	had started	before everyone arrived.

2. Many verbs have irregular past participles. Some of these end in *-en* (*taken, given, eaten, driven, written*, etc.) Others end in *-t* (*built, meant*, etc.) Common irregular past participles include *been, done, drunk, gone, read*, and *slept*.

> **TIP**
>
> Use Appendix 2 or your dictionary to make sure you have the correct form of the past participle.

USING THE PAST PERFECT

1. Use the past perfect to write about a past action or situation that happened before another past action. Use the simple past for the more recent action.

The rain had stopped by the time we left.

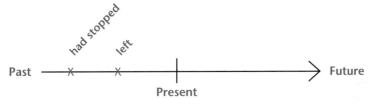

The students had read the book before they saw the movie.
     (first)   *(second)*

OR

Before they saw the movie, the students had read the book.
   (second)   *(first)*

2. Use the past perfect to write about an action or situation that happened before a specific time in the past.

> **Susan had never seen so many beautiful plants before that day.**
> **When the class ended, he had left already.**

3. Time words used in sentences with the past perfect include the following:

  before after until when by the time by then

> **Mrs. Long had gone to the theater *when* we called her.**
> **Jenny's parents had given her a car *by the time* she turned eighteen.**

> **TIP**
>
> Underline all time words in your writing, and make sure the verb tenses correspond to the time words.

4. The simple past can often replace the past perfect with no change in meaning.

> She went to dinner after she **had finished** the work.
>
> **OR**
>
> She went to dinner after she **finished** the work.

NOTE: When only one past event is mentioned in a sentence, use the simple past, not the past perfect.

> We **used** a dictionary during the test.
>
> **NOT**
> We had used a dictionary during the test.

SELF CHECK 3

Correct the errors in verb tense.

1. When the movie ended, Joan~~realized~~ (had) realized her friend left.

2. When she got to school, Grace ~~had~~ realized that she had left the house unlocked.

3. By the time our company offered him a job, John~~accepted~~ (had) accepted a position at another company.

4. We ~~had~~ attended the last class of the year yesterday.

5. The little boy ~~didn't see~~ (hadn't seen) a real lion before that day.

TIP

Wait several hours or days between writing and editing. This extra time will help you be more objective about your writing and see errors more clearly.

EDITING PRACTICE

1. *Put a check (✓) next to the sentences that use verb tenses correctly. Correct the sentences that have errors. Use the simple past, past progressive, or past perfect.*

____ 1. At age eleven, I understood the political situation in my country and why we have to move.

____ 2. She has gone to several concerts last month.

____ 3. When Brandon was a child, he would spend every summer sailing at the lake.

____ 4. When we first moved here, we had felt lonely.

____ 5. Lauren was taking the exam when, suddenly, she forgot all the answers.

____ 6. Her two cousins had seen the new play last night at the opening performance.

____ 7. My mother was preparing for Thanksgiving dinner at 11:30 last night.

____ 8. They had arrived in San Diego by the time I was getting there.

____ 9. My family was having three dogs and two cats at one time.

_____10. While they had lived in the mountains, they saw bears and mountain lions in their yard.

_____11. She was never taking a public speaking class before the one she took last semester.

_____12. Marty doesn't dance a lot now, but she used to be a professional dancer.

2 *In the following paragraph, the underlined verbs are not correct. Write the correct verb form above each underlined verb. Use the simple past, past progressive, or past perfect.*

My aunt is the best example I know of someone who is a hard worker. When she first arrived in the United States, she (1) doesn't know any English. She also knew very little regarding business in this country. She learned English while she (2) had taken business management classes. After school she (3) had studied. In addition, she worked at a small business in the evening. Because of all her hard work, she (4) was graduating with a business degree. She also (5) overcomed other difficulties. At that time, the economy (6) did poorly, and it was hard for her to find a job, but finally she (7) had found a good one. She worked at that job for five years. Then she (8) was quitting to take a better job. She started her new position last year, and after six months, her boss promoted her to an even better position. She (9) was being very happy with the promotion. My aunt is my role model because she pursued her goals even when all her effort (10) doesn't seem to pay off. Now she is successful and satisfied because all her hard work has been rewarded.

3 *Read the following paragraph. Complete the paragraph with the correct form of each verb given. Use the simple past or past progressive.*

At some point in life, most people can call themselves mature. I believe that I

_____matured_____ at a fairly young age. I _____became_____ mature the minute my family left our
  1. mature   **2. become**

country. We _____were flying_____ to the United States when my father told me it was my responsibility
         3. fly

to communicate in English for the family. I was only fourteen years old. Neither of my parents

spoke English, and five years ago, I _____knew_____ very little, but it was more English than
                                    4. know

anyone else in the family knew. For weeks, while my father _____was looking_____ for a place for us to
                                                           5. look

live, I had to do all of the talking for him. The day that my two younger sisters _____entered_____
                                                                                   6. enter

school, I _____was being_____ there to help them. Over the first few months, while my parents,
         7. be

grandmother, and siblings _____were adjusting_____ to our new home, I _____had_____ bigger things to
                          8. adjust   **9. have**

worry about. Although I _____learned_____ a lot, I wish that I had had a little longer to be a child.
                        10. learn

I definitely matured at a younger age than most people do.

4 *The following paragraph has ten errors in the use of past time tenses. Find and correct the errors.*

Today I still remembered the start of my longest friendship. It began in fourth grade. There was a girl in my class named Sandi. She was being the one who always forgot to raise her hand and who talked loudly to her friends. One day Sandi asked me to help her with her homework. I didn't want to help her, but I didn't know how to say no. I choosed not to answer her question. I was working quietly when she told the teacher I was her new homework partner. I disliked Sandi, and after a while I wasn't wanting to disregard her question. I had ignored her for as long as I could. I walked up to Sandi and told her I was not going to help with her homework. Nobody had ever said no to her before, so she was looking very surprised. The teacher had heard our conversation, and she came over to talk to me. She said that she needed my help with Sandi, so I had agreed to be her partner. After I have worked with Sandi for a few days, I was learning that she was very nice, and I judged her too quickly. It's amazing that we are still friends today when I think about how our friendship had started.

WRITING TOPICS

Choose one of the topics, and write at least one paragraph. Use mostly the past time tenses. After you complete your first draft, concentrate on editing your work. Keep in mind the editing practice from this chapter.

1. At some point in all of our lives, we leave home for the first time. Describe the first day you lived away from your home and your family. What was the day like, and how did you feel? Describe what you were doing before you left home.

2. Throughout our lives we are influenced by the people around us. Describe a time in your life when you were influenced by another person or group of people in either a positive or negative way. What was happening in your life at that time?

Go to page 88 for more practice with past time tenses.

CHAPTER 3

Subject-Verb Agreement

PRETEST

Check your understanding of subject-verb agreement. Put a check (✓) next to the sentences that are correct.

____ 1. India and China have the two fastest growing populations in the world.

____ 2. There are a lot of good movies that I want to see.

____ 3. Carrie and Kay is organizing the school elections.

____ 4. The elections was very successful last year.

____ 5. Do Ben live in a house or an apartment?

____ 6. Traveling to new cities are so much fun.

____ 7. My parents have contributed to my success in life.

____ 8. Our friend plays classical guitar beautifully.

____ 9. The Drama Department offer fun classes.

____ 10. One of her favorite flowers come from South America.

EDITING FOCUS

A verb must agree with its subject. It must agree in person (first person = *I*/*we*, second person = *you*, third person = *he, she, it, they*) and in number (singular or plural.) As writer and editor of your writing, you need to make sure the verbs agree with their subjects. Be especially careful deciding whether a subject is singular or plural.

Singular Subjects and Verbs	Plural Subjects and Verbs
I am studying.	We are studying.
You are studying.	You are studying.
He is studying.	They are studying.
His brother lives in Oregon.	The children live in Oregon.
It tastes good.	These strawberries taste good.
She works hard.	John and his brother work hard.

SUBJECT-VERB AGREEMENT IN DIFFERENT TENSES

Simple present	*Be:*
	I am ready.
	He / She / It is ready.
	We / You / They are ready.
	Regular verbs:
	I / You / We / They work.
	He / She / It works.
Present progressive	I am working.
	You / We / The boys are working.
	He / She / It is working.
Present perfect	I / You / We / They have eaten.
	He / She / It has eaten.

continued page 23

Simple past	**Be:**
	I / He / She / It was late.
	You / We / They were late.
	All other verbs:
	I / You / He / She / It / We / They worked.
Past progressive	**I / He / She / It was** eating
	You / We / They were eating

RULES FOR SUBJECT-VERB AGREEMENT

1. A verb must agree with its subject.

> Those **dogs are** really cute.

NOTE: The subject is not necessarily the noun nearest the verb.

> The **dogs** in that pet store window **are** really cute.

> **TIP**
>
> Underline the subjects and verbs in each sentence. Make sure that they agree.

2. When the subject is two or more nouns joined by *and,* use a plural verb.

> **Tacos and pizza have** always **been** my favorite foods.
> **Australia, Mexico, and France produce** delicious cheese.

3. If the subject of a sentence is *one of the* + plural noun, the main subject is *one* and the verb is singular.

> **One** of the students **has** the flu.

4. In sentences with *there + be,* the subject is the noun following *be.* If the noun is singular, use the singular form of *be.* If the noun is plural, use the plural form of *be.*

> There **is a show** on TV tonight that I really like to watch.
> There **has been** a lot of **crime** in our neighborhood recently.
> There **are ants** all over our kitchen.

5. Gerunds (verb + *-ing*) used as subjects take the third person singular form of the verb. (For more on gerunds, see Chapter 10.)

> For some people, **shopping** has become an obsession.
> **Discussing** politics **causes** arguments in many families.

EDITING PRACTICE

1 *Put a check (✓) next to the sentences that use subject-verb agreement correctly. Correct the sentences that have errors.*

_____ 1. When students has too much test anxiety, they don't perform well.

_____ 2. Having high-tech skills is useful in the workplace today.

_____ 3. The sofa and chair costs too much.

_____ 4. There is many times when I do not feel confident at school.

_____ 5. My family and I was happy when we left our war-torn country.

_____ 6. Some people take advantage of the welfare system while others use it responsibly.

_____ 7. New government policies requires businesses to pay more taxes.

_____ 8. What industries help strengthen the economy the most?

_____ 9. Having computer skills are not enough to succeed in a competitive work environment.

_____10. Oil prices goes down when there is a large oil supply.

_____11. One of the best children's stories are "Hansel and Gretel."

_____12. Jogging and swimming are good ways to stay fit.

2 *In the following paragraph, the underlined verbs are not correct. Write the correct verb form above each underlined verb.*

It is very important to understand the writing process. First, students need to think of themselves as writers, and practice good writing habits. After observing many of my friends, I **(1)** has found that there **(2)** is interesting characteristics many of them share. Most students in high school and college **(3)** is good writers when they want to be, but they usually **(4)** puts things off until the last minute. Then they don't have enough time to do a good job. Some students do the second draft immediately after the first, even though the teacher **(5)** ask for the drafts a week apart. Good writers use the first draft to explore ideas. They **(6)** waits a number of hours or days before beginning a second draft. Then they **(7)** becomes the editor and work at revising the ideas. A good essay **(8)** go through many revisions. One of the revision techniques that I find helpful **(9)** are asking another student to read the essay. All students should follow good writing habits to be the best writers they can be. Good writing and revising only **(10)** comes after a lot of time and practice.

3 *Read the following paragraph. Complete the paragraph with the correct form of each verb given.*

There _____ many qualities that make a good leader. It doesn't matter if the
        1. be

leader _____ in charge of a country, a high school, or a family. The same qualities
     2. be

_____ always necessary. Good leadership _____ flexibility, understanding,
   3. be   **4. require**

and honesty. Many people _____ some of these traits, but only a few have all of these
          5. have

traits plus the desire to be a great leader. Flexibility _____ one of the most important
                  6. be

qualities. Without the ability to adapt an idea or a plan to a specific situation, a leader will not

be successful. Along with flexibility, another important quality _____ understanding.
                             7. be

All outstanding leaders _____ the ability to put themselves into the shoes of others.
          8. have

Finally, in addition to flexibility and understanding, honesty _____ to be a part of
               9. have

a great leader's personality. We must be able to trust our leaders. Leaders that win our trust

are more successful than those who do not. Having these three qualities _____ what
                                   10. be

makes a leader great.

4 *The following paragraph has ten errors in subject-verb agreement. Find and correct the errors.*

When I first entered high school, I met my best friend for life, Chong. Throughout our

four years in high school, we was best friends. Now that we are away at different universities, our

friendship and affection has grown stronger. We communicates daily through e-mail. E-mail help

us stay in touch over a long distance. Chong is at the University of Chicago, and I am at the

University of Southern California, so it is difficult and expensive for us to communicate in any

other way. I think my best friend feel lonely in Illinois; therefore, I always takes the time to write

him. We have had many experiences together. One of the most memorable events were during our

senior year. It involved our senior physics final, which neither one of us did well on. There was

many times we competed against each other, but those times helped us to build a strong

friendship. I know Chong cherish our relationship as much as I do. We are both majoring in

biology and planning to go to the same medical school. Being apart now have made our

friendship stronger, and I'm sure our friendship will stay strong in the future.

WRITING TOPICS

Choose one of the topics, and write at least one paragraph. Use a variety of subjects, and make sure the subjects and verbs agree. After you complete your first draft, concentrate on editing your work. Keep in mind the editing practice from this chapter.

1. There are many beautiful places in the world, but everyone's idea of the most beautiful place is different. Some believe it is the beach, others say the mountains, while some think the desert or even the center of a big city is the most beautiful. In your opinion, what is the most beautiful place in the world? Describe this place, and explain why you think it is so beautiful.

2. People around the world celebrate many different holidays. We celebrate for a variety of reasons: religious, patriotic, romantic, historical, etc. What is your favorite holiday? In which country or countries is it celebrated? Why is this holiday important? What activities, people, food, and traditions are a part of the celebration?

Go to page 88 for more practice with subject-verb agreement.

Expressing Future Time

PRETEST

Check your understanding of verbs that express future time. Put a check (✓) next to the sentences that are correct.

____ 1. I won't register for the class unless you do.

____ 2. When Ti-lien will present her paper at the conference, she will use a computer.

____ 3. Our neighbor leaving for vacation this Saturday.

____ 4. Mr. Jackson gardens this afternoon.

____ 5. Ji promises that next year she will submit her taxes early.

____ 6. According to the weather report, it is raining on Friday.

____ 7. Dave and Kevin are going to watch their favorite TV show at 10:00 tonight.

____ 8. We buy a new house by next winter.

____ 9. He studies the formulas before he takes the exam next week.

____10. Before we cook dinner tonight, we are going to take a walk around the block.

EDITING FOCUS

There are four ways to express future time in English: with *will* + verb, *be going to* + verb, the simple present, and the present progressive. Each of these can be used to write about actions and situations that will happen at some time in the future. Although the forms share this general use, we use them in different situations. As writer and editor of your writing, you need to make sure that you choose the correct form.

Will	We **will get** there at about ten o'clock.
Be going to	I **am going to take** a class next month.
Present progressive	I **am eating** at Ki's house tonight.
Simple present	Our plane **leaves** at 5:00.

FORMING THE FUTURE

Will
Use *will* + the base form of the verb for all subjects. The negative form of *will* is *will not* or *won't*.

Subject	Verb	
I / You / He / She / It / We / They	will leave	next week.
I / You / He / She / It / We / They	will not leave / won't leave	next week.

Be going to
Use a simple present form of *be (am, is, are)* + *going to* + the base form of the verb.

Subject	Verb	
I	am going to finish	soon.
He / She / It	is going to finish	soon.
You / We / They	are going to finish	soon.

Present Progressive
Use a simple present form of *be* + the present participle (*-ing* form) of the verb. (For more on forming the present progressive, see Chapter 1.)

Simple Present
Add *-s* to the base form with third person singular subjects. Use the base form of the verb for all other subjects. (For more on forming the simple present, see Chapter 1.)

USING THE FUTURE FORMS

Will

- Use *will* to make **predictions** about the future.

    John **will win** the race.

- When you are less certain about a prediction, you can use a word such as *probably, maybe,* or *perhaps.*

    John **will** *probably* **win** the race.

    OR

    Maybe John **will win** the race.

- Use *will* to make **promises, offers,** and **requests**—that is, to talk about **willingness** to do something.

    I **will be** there. (promise)
    I**'ll take** you to the store if you need a ride. (offer)
    Will you **do** me a favor? (request)

NOTE: In a sentence about the future that has a time clause (a dependent clause beginning with a time word such as *after, before, when,* or *while*), use the simple present for the event in the time clause and use *will* or *be going to* for the event in the other clause.

    After Cindy **graduates,** she **will have** more time for her hobbies.

Be going to

- Use *be going to*, like *will,* to make **predictions** about the future.

    John **is going to win** the race.

- Use *be going to* to talk about **plans already made** for the future.

    I**'m going to have** dinner with Elena tomorrow night.

Present Progressive

The present progressive, like *be going to,* can be used to write about **plans already made** for the future.

    I**'m having** dinner with Elena tomorrow night.

NOTE: In future statements with *will, be going to,* or the present progressive where *and* is used to connect two actions for the same subject, it is not necessary to repeat the auxiliary verb.

    John **will win** the race and **come** home happy.
    I**'m going to have** dinner with Elena tomorrow night and **tell** her the good news.
    I**'m having** dinner with Elena tomorrow night and **telling** her about my new job.

Simple Present

Use the simple present to express future actions that are on a definite **schedule or timetable,** for example, movies, trains, etc. Verbs commonly used in the simple present to indicate the future include *arrive, begin, depart, finish, leave,* and *start.*

    This year school **starts** on September 3 and **finishes** on June 10.

Future Time Words

- Time words used with future time include the following:

  tonight   tomorrow   the day after tomorrow   later   next week

- When using the present progressive or simple present to express the future, use future time words to help make it clear that the event is in the future.

  Our flight leaves *next Saturday* **at 8:00** A.M.

> **TIP**
>
> Read all sentences in your essay aloud to make sure they make sense and don't sound awkward.

EDITING PRACTICE

① *Put a check (✓) next to the sentences that use verbs in future time correctly. Correct the sentences that have errors. Use* will, be going to, *simple present, or present progressive.*

_____ 1. Next summer I'm going to enroll in a language class.

_____ 2. After she graduates, Anna gets a part-time job, which will be a good experience for her.

_____ 3. I think that this class will be very interesting, but we have a lot of homework.

_____ 4. The president of the company is at the meeting tomorrow.

_____ 5. We can't wait to see our friends who are going arrive on the next flight.

_____ 6. Tomorrow the bus leaves at 7:00 P.M.

_____ 7. After I work hard all day, I will sleeping like a baby.

_____ 8. We are remembering to pick you up at the airport next week.

_____ 9. They willn't work at the same place they worked last year.

_____ 10. Some of my friends from Taiwan are coming to visit me next spring.

_____ 11. Melissa will rents a house in the mountains for her vacation next year.

_____ 12. When my parents will arrive, we are going to take them out for dinner.

② *In the following essay, ten of the underlined verbs are not correct. Write the correct form above each underlined verb. Use* will, be going to, *the simple present, or the present progressive. In some cases, more than one future form is correct.*

This summer vacation (1) <u>is going to be</u> the best vacation of my life. Four of my friends

and I are planning to visit Korea for one month. I am really excited about this trip because it

(2) <u>will be</u> the first time I've traveled without my family. In addition to visiting our old friends,

we have planned a lot of fun activities. First we (3) <u>arriving</u> in Seoul and (4) <u>stay</u> with my cousins for three weeks. While we (5) <u>will be</u> in Seoul, we (6) <u>are going to shop</u>, eat delicious food, and just hang out with our friends until very late at night. Clothing and appearance are important in a big cosmopolitan city, so we (7) <u>are looking</u> very fashionable when we (8) <u>go</u> downtown. The weather is very hot in Korea in the summer, so it is not a good idea to spend a lot of time outside. This is why most of our adventures in Seoul (9) <u>willn't include</u> many outdoor activities but (10) <u>will include</u> places with air conditioning! After we (11) <u>will leave</u> Seoul, we (12) <u>are going stay</u> with some friends for a week in the countryside. Korea has some of the most beautiful mountain scenery in the world. Hopefully, the mountains (13) <u>are</u> cool, so we can go hiking and exploring.

After one month in Korea, I (14) <u>will return</u> home to find a job. I (15) <u>will probably have</u> about six weeks to earn some money to help pay for my school tuition. Even though working is not as much fun as traveling in Korea, I know that this summer I (16) <u>contribute</u> to my education by earning some money. I plan to work for my aunt's company because I (17) <u>will gain</u> a lot of useful experience there. This type of business experience (18) <u>will helps</u> me when I start to look for a real job in a few years, after I (19) <u>will graduate</u>.

3 *Read the following essay. Choose the verb that best completes each sentence, and write it on the line.*

Many schools, colleges, and universities have beautiful architecture and interesting sights to see, yet their campuses are sometimes overwhelming because they are so big and unfamiliar to visitors. I always tell new students that I _____ them on a walking tour of our school
1. take / will take
so that they'll feel more comfortable here. My family is coming to visit me next weekend. Their plane _____ in on Saturday morning. They _____ a car to get here from
2. getting / gets   **3. rent / are renting**
the airport.

This is how I _____ them the campus. My family is going to enter at the main
4. will show / show
gate on the western side of the campus. After they enter the main gate, they _____ a
5. see / will see
big parking lot for visitors. When they _____ the parking lot, they will see me standing
6. will exit / exit
by the statue of the university's first chancellor. Here they will see the most famous building on

campus, the admissions building, which was built in the late 1800s. Its beautiful architecture makes it one of the most impressive buildings on campus. I predict this _____ their

7. is / will be

favorite place on the campus. Directly across from the admissions building and through the park, my family will see where I spend all of my time, the science plaza with its chemistry, biology, and physics buildings. We will follow the sidewalk behind the science plaza to the main library. A new arboretum is being developed there, on the empty land behind the library. Even though the university _____ building the arboretum for another few

8. doesn't finish / won't finish

months, I know my father _____ to spend some time there. The botany

9. is wanting / will want

department has wonderful greenhouses that we _____ after we leave the

10. tour / are going to tour

library. After visiting the greenhouses and before leaving the university, my little brother and sister _____ at the student store, where they can buy books, clothing, and

11. are going to stop / stop

many other items related to the university. I think that this tour _____ my family see

12. helps / will help

how I spend my days on campus. I definitely suggest it for any first-time visitors.

4 *The following essay has ten errors in the use of future time forms. Find and correct the errors. There may be more than one way to correct some errors.*

           My friends and I are beginning [will begin] to think seriously about what we are going to do after we finish our last English class. We definitely know what we are doing right after we take our last exam; it's the distant future that is more uncertain! Immediately after we finish our last exam, a big group of us will walks [is going to walk] to the nearest arcade to celebrate. The owner has promised us that his arcade will be [is being to] a good place to start our celebration. We spend an hour or two at the arcade before we go to the next event. Koko and Elena have a party and dinner at their apartment. When we get there, we go [are going to] swimming, play darts, horseshoes, and cards, and eat delicious food from all over the world. Each person will bring one dish from his or her country. This way, the food is tasting [will taste] exotic. We all know that this is a great party and a wonderful way to end our studies together, but there are big questions about our futures that we still need to answer.

           After I will [ ] say good-bye to all of my friends at the party, I am going home to pack my bags. I will leave the following day for my next adventure. Even though I wiln't [don't] know exactly what I am going [will] do in my uncle's company until I arrive, I plan to use my newly improved English skills. My uncle wants me to work with his English-speaking suppliers and customers since he does not feel comfortable speaking in his second language. My future home ~~will~~ *is going to* be on another continent. This will be the third I have lived on. I think that I *will* love it as much as the first two.

WRITING TOPICS

Choose one of the topics, and write at least one paragraph. Try to use all the future time forms. After you complete your first draft, concentrate on editing your work. Keep in mind the editing practice from this chapter.

1. In fifty years, our world will probably be a very different place to live. What do you predict the world will be like in 50 years? Describe areas you feel relatively certain about as well as those you are not so certain about. Some things you might want to think about are the environment, technology, business, government, and family life.

2. Select a building, a park, a city, or any other place that you are very familiar with. Pretend that you are taking a group of friends there for the first time. Think about what your friends will do while they are there and how you hope they will feel about this place when they leave.

Go to page 89 for more practice expressing future time.

CHAPTER 5

Time Shifts and Tense

PRE**TEST**

Check your understanding of time shifts and tense. Put a (✓) next to the sentences that are correct.

___✓___ 1. Before he buys a computer, he will look for the best price.

_____ 2. The conference always began May 1, so I will arrive April 30.

_____ 3. Piano music is so beautiful that I decide to take lessons.

_____ 4. I have seen my favorite movie, which is *The Sound of Music,* for the first time in fifth grade.

_____ 5. Helen is at the gym now, but she is home soon.

_____ 6. We don't see the car you bought last month yet.

___✓___ 7. Sonja looked embarrassed when she fell on the library stairs.

_____ 8. Mollie was taking a film studies class this semester, so she went to the movies last night for homework.

_____ 9. Economists believe unemployment will increase next year.

_____ 10. Jack is finishing cleaning his room, but his mother thought it still wasn't clean enough.

EDITING FOCUS

Writers often shift between past, present, and future time. In order for your reader to understand these time shifts, it is important to choose tenses carefully and to use tenses and time words together correctly.

USING TIME SHIFTS AND TENSE

1. The example paragraph below is mainly about present time. Notice how the tenses change and how time words show these changes.

> (1) *These days* many of the teachers at our school **are struggling** to control their classes. (2) Teachers **feel** that their students **don't respect** them. (3) In the end, they **say**, this **makes** them less successful as teachers. (4) What **is going on**? (5) *Several months ago*, a school committee **asked** students to describe successful teachers. (6) The students' responses **were** very interesting. (7) In their responses, students **emphasized** the importance of control and also of a challenging curriculum. (8) These responses **confirm** that we **need** to look more closely at the issue of classroom control and perhaps at our curriculum as well. (9) We **have to take** these problems seriously *now*, so they **will not become** worse *in the future*.

NOTE: This paragraph is mainly about the present situation in the school. However, sentences 5–7 switch to the past to talk about student responses from several months ago, and the second part of sentence 9 switches to the future.

2. The example paragraph below is mainly about past time. Notice how the tenses change and how time words show these changes.

> (1) *Two months ago*, in a suburban school, students **beat up** a substitute teacher and *afterward* **didn't seem** to feel sorry about what they **had done**. (2) Apparently, the substitute **had been** unable to control the class. (3) The incident, which **began** when several boys **jumped** on the teacher's desk, **ended** only when the principal and security **arrived**. (4) The school **suspended** the boys for the rest of the year. (5) Unfortunately, *in recent years* this type of incident **has become** more common.

NOTE: This paragraph is mainly about an incident that happened two months ago. However, sentence 5 switches to the present to indicate that this incident is part of a general trend in recent years.

CHOOSING TENSES AND TIME WORDS

1. Use the correct tense for the time you are talking about. Make sure the tenses you choose make sense together. Compare statements (A) and (B). Statement (A) shifts from the present to the past to the future, and statement (B) is all about the past.

        simple present   simple past   future

(A) I'm tired *today* because I **didn't sleep** much *last night*. I'll **go** to bed early *tonight*.

          simple past   past perfect   simple past

(B) I **was** tired *yesterday* because I **hadn't slept** much *the night before*, so I **went** to bed early *last night*.

2. Use time words that relate to the time you are writing about. They must fit with the tenses you use.

- Present time words/phrases: *today, (right) now, at the present,* and *currently.* (See also Chapter 1.)

  My family **lives** in California *now*.

- Past time words/phrases: *yesterday, last night/week/month/year,* and *ago.* (See also Chapter 2.)

  The prime minister **addressed** parliament *last night*.

- Future time words/phrases: *tomorrow, next week/month/year,* and *in the future.* (See also Chapter 4.)

  We **will have** our last final *tomorrow*.

3. To help readers follow your writing, use time words to signal shifts in time.

  I **saw** a doctor about my allergies *last month*, and *now* I'm **sneezing** a lot less.
  Last year the government **placed** ten new animals on the endangered species list.
  Unfortunately, this list **has grown** longer *in recent years*.

> **TIP**
>
> In all of your writing, check for appropriate time shifts by underlining time expressions and making sure they correspond to the verb tenses that are used in each sentence.

EDITING PRACTICE

1 *Put a check (✓) next to the sentences that use tenses and time words correctly. Correct the sentences that have errors.*

____ 1. Their relationship has been better since they return from vacation last month.

____ 2. The Martins are living in Australia now and will move to New Zealand later this year.

____ 3. May's father hasn't seen the grades that she receives on her last report card.

____ 4. At first we only studied grammar and vocabulary, but now we are using the grammar and vocabulary to write paragraphs.

____ 5. According to anthropologists, in prehistoric times women prepare the food while men protected the camp.

____ 6. In an unfair political system, the wealthiest people benefit and other citizens didn't.

____ 7. In the next century, technology will be more secure than it is now.

____ 8. I had a bad headache for two hours; I'm going to take some aspirin.

____ 9. Most Americans nowadays didn't remember the reasons for the Memorial Day holiday, which they celebrate every May.

____ 10. The second-grade students visited the school's garden last week, and they are currently learning about the plants that they saw.

____11. Joy and Joe are going to buy the new house that is on the corner.

____12. Sonja still has the first bicycle that her parents buy her.

2 *In the following paragraph, the underlined verbs are not correct. Write the correct verb tense above each underlined verb.*

Even though it has been ten years since I last visited my grandfather's home, I (1) knew that it hasn't changed at all. My cousin's letters describe the house the way I still see it in my memory. Grandfather's house sits on the corner of a small street and has a large front gate with several trees that are standing like guards in front of a palace. The front door is bright red and (2) had a mail slot in the middle of it. A twelve-foot-high fence (3) surrounded the entire house. In the front courtyard, the smell of beautiful flowers (4) overpowered anyone who enters. Whenever I smell those flowers today, the fragrance reminds me of the happy times I (5) spend at the house as a child. Ten years ago when I (6) live in the town near my grandfather's, my father (7) takes us to visit him almost every weekend. When we got there, we (8) enter the house through the side door before my grandfather knew we (9) are there, and we surprised him with our entrance. I still (10) remembered that time vividly. These are special memories that I will keep forever.

3 *Read the following essay. Complete the essay with the simple present, simple past, or future form of each verb given. Use the time words as clues.*

A few years ago when I _____ in high school, I _____ with the
                         1. be   **2. practice**
marching band every morning on the football field at 7:00. The band had to finish practice

by 8:00 A.M. because the sprinklers _____ to water the field, and we _____
                                     3. begin   **4. want, not**
to go to our first class all wet! While we were practicing, the other students _____
                                                                                  5. start
to arrive. This _____ still my strongest high school memory because band practice
                 6. be

_____ the happiest part of my four years at University High School. I _____
 7. be   **8. love**
playing in the band, and I _____ so many good friends. We _____ still good
                           9. make   **10. be**
friends today, and I _____ that we _____ friends forever.
                      11. hope   **12. remain**

Today, University High _____ the largest high school in town with over 3,500

13. be

students. The campus _____ many large two-story buildings, a football field,

14. have

gymnasium, auditorium, several computer and science labs, and many more facilities. The school

now _____ several blocks in the downtown area, a space that was mostly field not so

15. take up

long ago. The area is growing so fast that the school _____ nearly 4,000 students next

16. have

year. It isn't exactly the school I _____ to all those years ago, but it still _____

17. go   **18. hold**

many happy memories for me.

4 *The following paragraph has ten errors in the use of verb tense. Use the time words to help you
find and correct the errors.*

Many people are *now* adopting children who are five years old or older from former

Soviet countries that can no longer care for their orphans and disabled children. *In the past,* I

always plan to adopt an infant. I *still* thought adopting poor and mistreated children is a

humanitarian thing to do; however, I am *now* getting a sense of the large sacrifices involved in

adopting a child. *A few months ago,* my neighbors adopted a seven-year-old boy from Romania.

Before I met their new son, I believe he was going to be happy to have kind and loving parents.

However, *now* I am not so certain. He doesn't know how to respond to love because he never

receives any *in the first few years of his life. By the time he was five,* he develops his own thoughts

and behaviors that were appropriate for a child in his situation. In his *current* place in a loving

family, these thoughts and behaviors were not appropriate. The child is slowly adapting to his new

environment, and I am sure in the *next few years* he grows familiar with his new family members

and surroundings. I *now* see the unique challenges that adopted children brought to families. I *still*

believe children are wonderful, and they increased the joy in their parents' lives, but *sometimes*

adopting children led to unforeseen problems.

WRITING TOPICS

Choose one of the topics, and write at least one paragraph. Think carefully about the times you will write about. Use time words to signal time shifts, and use tenses and time words together appropriately. After you complete your first draft, concentrate on editing your work. Keep in mind the editing practice from this chapter.

1. Describe the most memorable event from your childhood or adolescence. Why was this event significant? How did it change you or the way you think? How are you different today because of this event?

2. In many families, the parents have specific plans for their children's lives and careers. Do you think it is better for children to follow their parents' plan or their own? What plan did your parents have for you when you were a child or a younger student? Have you followed this plan so far? Will you follow this plan in the future? Why or why not?

Go to page 89 for more practice with time shifts and tense.

CHAPTER 6

Count and Noncount Nouns

PRE**TEST**

Check your understanding of count and noncount nouns. Put a check (✓) next to the sentences that are correct.

_____ 1. Please help me correct the grammars in my paper.

_____ 2. The parks in our city are full of birds.

_____ 3. Last night Lisa wrote a six-pages research paper.

_____ 4. My friends want to have four childrens.

_____ 5. We have been to the museum four time.

_____ 6. Did the traffics slow you down today?

_____ 7. Our pet bird has a broken leg.

_____ 8. All the houses on our block have been broken into by thiefs.

_____ 9. Would you rather plant flowers or fruit in the garden?

_____ 10. I prefer taking a vacations on my birthday to receiving gifts.

EDITING FOCUS

There are two categories of nouns in English: count nouns and noncount nouns. There are several differences between these two categories, so it is important for you to consider which nouns are count and which are noncount in your writing.

COUNT NOUNS

1. Count nouns are nouns that can be counted (e.g., *school: a school, one school, two schools,* etc.) Because count nouns can be counted, they have singular and plural forms (e.g., *school* and *schools*). Singular count nouns take singular verb forms, and plural count nouns take plural verb forms.

2. Regular plurals are generally formed by adding *-s*.

> student → students   book → books

3. Spelling changes are required in some cases.
If a noun ends in *-ch, -sh, -s,* or *-x,* add *-es*.

> patch → patches   class → classes

If a noun ends in a consonant + *-y,* change *-y* to *-i* and add *-es*.

> baby → babies   lady → ladies

If a noun ends in *-f* or *-fe,* drop the *-f* or *-fe* and add *-ves*.

> leaf → leaves   wife → wives

If a noun ends in a vowel + *-o,* add *-s*.

> radio → radios

If a noun ends in a *consonant* + *-o,* add *-es*.

> tomato → tomatoes

4. Some plural count nouns are irregular; they do not take the *-s* ending.

Singular	Plural
child	children
woman	women
person	people
foot	feet
phenomenon	phenomena

> **TIP**
> When using a new noun, refer to a dictionary if you are unsure of its plural form.

5. If a noun is used to modify another noun (if it is used as an adjective), it is always singular.

> We have to read a seven-**chapter** book by tomorrow.
> My **book** club meets on Wednesdays.

SELF CHECK 1

Correct the errors involving count nouns.

1. His brother has two lab in the Biology Department this quarter.

2. The class had to write a five-paragraphs paper.

3. Earthquakes and hurricanes are horrible tragedys.

4. The lecture was presented by two mans from the Department of Energy.

5. The soccer team had two matchs last week.

NONCOUNT NOUNS

1. Noncount nouns are nouns that cannot be counted (e.g., *intelligence, meat, love*). Because these nouns cannot be counted, they generally cannot be made plural.

> **TIP**
>
> Languages differ in whether a noun is considered count or noncount. If you are not sure whether a noun is count or noncount in English, look it up in your dictionary. An ESL dictionary such as the *Longman Dictionary of American English* will indicate whether nouns are count (C) or noncount (N). Noncount is also called uncountable (U).

2. Many noncount nouns fit into categories. Here are some examples:

Foods	bread, cheese, meat, sugar
Liquids	coffee, gasoline, milk, paint, water, wine
Solids	glass, ice, paper, wood
Gases	air, oxygen, smog
Particles	dust, sand
Natural phenomena	light, rain, thunder, weather
Groups of similar items	clothing, equipment, furniture, jewelry, junk, luggage, mail, makeup, money, stuff, traffic, vocabulary
Abstract ideas	advice, anger, beauty, employment, enjoyment, freedom, fun, hate, honesty, information, intelligence, knowledge, love, luck, news, patience, research, sadness, work
Activities	(*expressed with gerunds*) reading, swimming, writing
Fields of study	chemistry, literature, physics, psychology, mathematics, economics

3. If the subject of the sentence is a noncount noun, use a singular verb.

> **Good luck comes in many forms.**
> **Smog is sometimes a threat to people's health.**

NOTE: Even if a noncount noun ends in *-s*, use a singular verb.

> **Physics is my favorite subject.**

4. The articles *a/an* cannot be used with noncount nouns.

> **I'm going to ask my uncle for advice.**
>
> **NOT**
> **I'm going to ask my uncle for an advice.**

SELF CHECK 2

Correct the errors involving noncount nouns. If necessary, change the verb form.

1. We learned new vocabularies last week.

2. The weathers at the beach are usually sunny.

3. My mother loves to drink coffees every morning.

4. The professor did a lot of researches with her graduate students.

5. I found some good informations on the Internet.

TIP

Try editing your essay by reading it backwards from the last paragraph to the first. By reading the paragraphs out of the expected order, you may notice errors that you don't see when you read the essay in the usual way.

EDITING PRACTICE

1 *Put a check (✓) next to the sentences that use count and noncount nouns correctly. Correct the sentences that have errors.*

____ 1. We sold all of our furniture at the garage sale and made $400.

____ 2. Our employer makes us do a lot of works.

____ 3. The research was inconsistent with the current theory.

____ 4. I would like a bread and a piece of cheese.

____ 5. In non-traditional families, the wifes work while the husbands stay at home.

____ 6. My daughter is levelheaded and has two foots on the ground.

____ 7. World music is growing in popularity.

_____ 8. There was too much cars on the road this morning.

_____ 9. I need to buy two loaves of bread for dinner.

_____ 10. Many old homes have ten-feet ceilings.

2 *In the following paragraph, the underlined nouns are not correct. Write the correct noun form above each underlined noun.*

When (1) <u>peoples</u> make a broad or oversimplified generalization, this statement is

called a stereotype. Almost everyone is familiar with some stereotypes. For example, *athletes are*

dumb and *students interested in computers are nerds* are just two of many common (2) <u>stereotype</u>.

One of the richest sources for stereotypes is the state of California. People say that everyone

in California surfs, eats health food, and has a tan. They all have blond (3) <u>hairs</u>, too. Although

the previous (4) <u>statement</u> may be funny, sometimes stereotypes are unkind and cause a group of

people (5) <u>sadnesses</u>. Therefore, whenever possible, it is important to be aware of oversimplified

(6) <u>generalization</u>. (7) <u>Informations</u> and (8) <u>educations</u> are the best ways to avoid stereotyping

and the problems associated with it.

3 *Read the following paragraph. Complete the paragraph with the nouns given. Make them plural or leave them unchanged when necessary.*

It is a tradition in many families that high school seniors receive presents for graduation.

Many students are lucky enough to get _____ or nice _____. After listening
                                              1. money   **2. jewelry**

to the _____ of several of my older friends and siblings, I decided what I really wanted
        3. advice

for my high school graduation gift was a long vacation in Mexico, so I could visit all of my

_____. _____ and _____ in a foreign country were the things I
   4. relative   **5. excitement**   **6. travel**

longed for. I was lucky to receive some new _____ from my grandmother and the
                                                7. luggage

airline and train _____ from my parents. I had a wonderful summer in my native
                    8. ticket

country and took many nice _____ to the beach and surrounding areas. I hope to
                              9. trip

return many _____ in the future, and I thank my parents for their memorable
              10. time

graduation gift to me.

4 *The following paragraph has ten errors in the use of count and noncount nouns. Find and correct the errors.*

While I was in high school, I was lucky to have many good friend. Unfortunately, some of my friends eventually became more like enemies. During our freshman and sophomore years, there were five of us who shared secrets and never spent a minute apart. We all became friends in our ninth-grade English class because we liked to study grammars and read the five-hundred-pages novels that the teacher always assigned. I thought we would be friends forever; however, I was wrong. It started with three argument between two friends who always thought only of themselves and wouldn't share anything—not even clothings. These disagreement forced our group to split in half by the end of our junior year. I learned many lessons from this experience. One of the things I will always remember is the importance of honesties. Friends must tell each other the truths. If they tell lies, the friendships that they share will not last. Now I have a new group of five friend in college, and I hope these new friendships will last forever. It is impossible for friends to avoid trouble all of the time, but I know the pain of losing friend and will do anything to keep my new group together.

WRITING TOPICS

Choose one of the topics, and write at least one paragraph. Use singular and plural count nouns as well as noncount nouns. After you complete your first draft, concentrate on editing your work. Keep in mind the editing practice from this chapter.

1. What is your favorite food? How do you prepare it? What ingredients are needed to make it? Do you consider this dish spicy, mild, or exotic? What is it that you like best about this food? Is it prepared for special occasions?

2. We all experience new and sometimes difficult situations in life that are easier to deal with if we don't feel alone. When you encounter one of these situations, who do you talk to about it? Why do you choose to talk to this person? Describe the traits that draw you to him or her and make you feel comfortable talking about your problems.

Go to page 90 for more practice with count and noncount nouns.

CHAPTER 7

Articles and Other Determiners

PRETEST

Check your understanding of articles and determiners. Put a check (✓) next to the sentences that are correct.

_____ 1. That's best book I've ever read.

_____ 2. Do you want to go to a movie tonight? I don't care which one.

_____ 3. How was a lecture yesterday on photosynthesis?

_____ 4. Her kids left sand all over the car after going to the beach.

_____ 5. We have to return this books to the library.

_____ 6. I was so full after lunch that I didn't eat any dinner.

_____ 7. Jan bought several new CDs yesterday.

_____ 8. We didn't find much antiques that we liked at the auction.

_____ 9. Caroline and Rich said they would take the bike ride later today.

_____ 10. Dan recognized a little songs at the concert.

EDITING FOCUS

Determiners go before nouns. There are four kinds of determiners:

- articles (*a, an, the*)
- quantifiers (*a lot of, a few,* etc.)
- demonstrative adjectives (*this, that, these, those*)
- possessive adjectives (*my, your,* etc.)

In order to know which determiner to use, you need to know whether the noun is count or noncount (see Chapter 6). You also need to know whether you are referring to a noun in general or to a specific noun. When you write and edit, make sure the determiners you use are appropriate for the meaning you want to communicate and for the nouns that go with them.

Article	**The** train is late.
Quantifier	I need **a few** minutes to finish.
Demonstrative adjective	I'm enrolled in **that** class.
Possessive adjective	**My** friend is going to help me.

ARTICLES

A, An, AND *The*

1. Use *a/an* (the indefinite article) with singular count nouns to express general meaning.
Use *a* or *an* when the thing you are referring to is not specific, and the reader does not know to which particular thing you are referring.

> I bought **a** book last night. *(We don't know what book.)*

Use *a* before a noun beginning with a consonant sound (*a boy, a hunter, a university,* etc.).
Use *an* before a noun beginning with a vowel sound (*an apple, an honor,* etc.).

> My parents bought me **a** bicycle.
> You should bring **an** umbrella.

A noncount noun usually cannot occur with *a/an.*

> **Work** gives us satisfaction and brings in money.
>
> NOT
> A work gives us satisfaction and brings in money.

A singular count noun is always preceded by *a/an, the,* or another determiner (see pages 49–51).

> I ate **an/the/your** apple.
>
> NOT
> I ate apple.

2. No article (also known as Ø or *zero article*) is used with plural count nouns and noncount nouns to express general meaning.

> **Movies** are my favorite form of entertainment.
> I think that **honesty** is important.

Generally, do not use an article with names of people, places, and things (also called *proper nouns*). Sometimes, however, *the* is part of the name.

> **Luis** is originally from **Caracas, Venezuela**, but he now lives in **the** United States.

3. *The* (the definite article) is used to express specific meaning with all three kinds of nouns—singular count, plural count, and noncount. In this case, the reader knows to which particular thing you are referring.

> **The** assignment in art history is interesting. *(We know which it is.)*
> **The** door was locked. *(The door was previously mentioned or is the only door.)*
> **The** trains are often crowded at this time of day.
> He gave us **the** information that we needed.

4. Use the definite article *the* in the following cases:
   - with superlatives (*the best, the cheapest, the most, the least,* etc.; see Chapter 11)

> **The fastest** runner finished in less than two minutes.

   - with ordinal numbers (*the first, the second, the third,* etc.)

> I didn't understand **the second** question on the test.

   - with *same*

> Dora and I have **the same** hairstyle.
> She made **the same** mistakes as I did.

5. In general, select *a/an* or no article when using a noun for the first time and *the* (or another determiner) every time afterwards.

> I put **a** book in your room. *(indefinite—what book?)*
> **The** book is on your desk. *(definite—the book I put in your room)*
> We saw **a** good movie at the university center last night. **The** movie was about space aliens.
> We bought furniture last night. **The** furniture will be delivered tomorrow.

SUMMARY OF ARTICLE USAGE

Use the diagram to help you decide which articles to use with nouns.

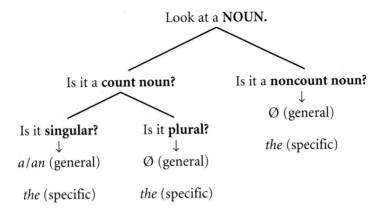

> **TIP**
>
> If you can't decide whether or not a noun needs an article, refer to the diagram to help you.

SELF CHECK 1

Correct the errors involving articles.

1. My sister read the good book last week.

2. I took an exam yesterday. An exam was hard.

3. Albert Einstein had intelligence necessary to transform the twentieth century.

4. Parents teach their children about the life.

5. I think I answered last question incorrectly.

OTHER DETERMINERS

QUANTIFIERS

1. Use quantifiers before nouns to indicate an amount or number.

   We brought two books and several magazines.

2. Quantifiers that can be used with plural count nouns include the following:

   few   a few   several   some   many   a lot of / lots of

   I had several questions about the article we read.

   Note the difference between the use of *few* and *a few:*

Few people came to the party.	Meaning: We expected more people.
A few people stayed late.	Meaning: Some, or a small number of people, stayed late.

3. Quantifiers that can be used with noncount nouns include the following:

     little   a little   some   much   a lot of / lots of

Note the difference between the use of *little* and *a little:*

> **He gave me little help.**   Meaning: He didn't give me enough help.
> **He gave me a little help.**   Meaning: He gave me some, or a small amount of, help.

4. *Some* is often replaced by *any* in questions and negative statements.

> **Did you have any problems with the assignment?**
> **No, I didn't have any problems. / Yes, I had some problems.**

5. *Much* is often used with noncount nouns in questions and negative statements. It is unusual in affirmative statements. Use *a lot (of)* instead of *much* in affirmative statements.

> **Did you get much sleep last night?**
> **No, I didn't get much sleep. / Yes, I got a lot of sleep.**

6. *Each* and *every* are followed by singular count nouns + singular verbs.

> **Every student meets with an adviser once a year.**
> **Each university charges a different amount for room and board.**

Each of and *one of* + *the* are followed by a plural count noun. The verb remains singular.

> **Each of the students plans to take the test.**
> **One of the students isn't finished yet.**

DEMONSTRATIVE ADJECTIVES

Use the demonstrative adjectives *this* and *that* with singular count nouns and with noncount nouns. Use *these* and *those* with plural count nouns.

> **This test is the hardest that I've ever taken.**
> **That furniture seems just right for your house.**
> **These courses are at the introductory level.**
> **Did you pay a lot of money for those clothes?**

POSSESSIVE ADJECTIVES

The following are the possessive adjectives:

     my   your   his   her   its   our   their

Use possessive adjectives before a noun. They can be used with any kind of noun.

> **My parents live in Venezuela.**
> **We need to include their information in the report.**

NOTE: Don't confuse the possessive adjective *its* with *it's*, the contraction of *it is.*

> **Its writing program is very well known. It's (it is) among the best in the country.**

ANOTHER, OTHER

1. Use *another* with singular count nouns. It means "one in addition to the one(s) already mentioned."

   My older brother lives in Los Angeles, and I have another brother living in New York.

2. Use *other* with plural count nouns and with noncount nouns. It means "more or several more in addition to the one(s) already mentioned."

   I've already finished, and other students have finished, too. *(some in addition to me, but not all)*
   He did other research that supports these results.

3. Use *the other* with singular or plural count nouns. It means "the rest of a specific group."

   I've already finished, and the other student has finished, too.
   I've already finished, and the other students have finished, too. *(all the students have finished)*

SELF CHECK 2

Correct the errors involving determiners.

1. The anthropology class took each tests in the large lecture hall.

2. We didn't buy many clothing at the mall.

3. We didn't see some wildflowers on our nature walk.

4. Each of the sociology test is worth 100 points.

5. Can I make an appointment on other day?

> **TIP**
>
> Use the *edit-find* function on your computer to check for specific punctuation, words, or expressions that may cause problems. For example, use the computer to find all uses of *a* or *an*, so you can check that they are used correctly.

EDITING PRACTICE

1 *Put a check (✓) next to the sentences that use articles and other determiners correctly. Correct the sentences that have errors.*

____ 1. I hope that I can get better grade on the next quiz.

____ 2. They arrived a few weeks after the Thanksgiving.

____ 3. There wasn't much news today.

____ 4. We get homework in every classes.

_____ 5. Each student has to do an oral presentation.

_____ 6. These test is difficult for students who have recently started to learn English.

_____ 7. I completely understand the directions. I don't have some questions.

_____ 8. She wants an ice in her drink.

_____ 9. This author has just written other book that you should read.

_____10. Each one of the teacher is giving us a test next week.

2 *In the following paragraph, five of the underlined phrases have errors in the use of nouns and determiners. Write your corrections above each underlined phrase.*

I am living with several roommates for (1) the first time, and I now know that there are

(2) morning personalities and (3) night personalities. There are people who wake up without

(4) alarm clock at 7:00 A.M. and are ready to face the day with a smile. However, (5) the same people

are asleep by 10:00 P.M. Then there are others who come to life at 10:00 P.M. but don't roll out

of bed until noon or later. Everyone has energy at different times of the day. (6) Each roommates

in my house has a different body clock. Sometimes (7) these difference can make living together

(8) a problem. We have had (9) a few disagreements because of stereos, phones, and alarms going off

at unreasonable times of the day and night. The most important lesson we all have had to learn is

(10) the patience. Patience and communication are the only ways we will be able to remain friends

over the course of (11) this year. Living with roommates has certainly opened (12) mine eyes

to various lifestyles and sleeping patterns!

3 *Read the following paragraph. Complete the paragraph with* a, the, *or* Ø *(no article).*

Living in _____ new country is always an adventure. There are so many
    1. a / the / Ø

different customs that one must get used to in order to feel comfortable. This happened to me

when I was _____ foreign exchange student for one year in _____ France.
    2. a / the / Ø   3. a / the / Ø

There were a lot of things that were unusual at first but became natural after _____
                                                                              4. a / the / Ø

few months. After returning to _____ United States, one of _____ most
                                5. a / the / Ø   6. a / the / Ø

interesting things I noticed was how strange customs are here! I never questioned these customs before I lived in France, but after living in the new culture, I became much more aware. When

I moved back home, _____ tipping was _____ first custom that struck

               7. a / the / Ø   **8. a / the / Ø**

me as strange. Another thing that I had to get used to again was _____ traffic in my

                                                                  9. a / the / Ø

hometown. American drivers, however, have _____ patience with traffic, whereas

                                         10. a / the / Ø

French drivers do not. The part of American culture that I now find sad is _____ lack

                                                               11. a / the / Ø

of extended family living nearby or in the same house. I observed French family life while I was

living in a French home. _____ family that I lived with had grandparents as well as a

                          12. a / the / Ø

few aunts and cousins in _____ same house. It was so nice to have family members

                        13. a / the / Ø

close by. _____ experiences that I had while living abroad have given me more insights

               14. a / the / Ø

into life in the United States and in Europe.

4 *The following paragraph has ten errors in the use of articles and other determiners. Find and correct the errors. There may be more than one way to correct some errors.*

      We have all been exposed to much teachers throughout our lives. These teachers come

in many forms: schoolteachers, parents, relatives, friends, and neighbors. There are many

aspects to being a good teacher. One important job of all teachers is building self-confidence,

and other job is motivating the students. A lot of students have been motivated by a teacher

during their lives. Giving a praise is one of the most successful ways to help students learn.

However, each teachers has a unique style for motivating students. Most "A" students

are self-motivated or are motivated by good grade. The remaining students need a few

encouragement from their teachers. Students spend so much time with them that they need

a teachers to speak kindly and give them guidance. My favorite elementary school teacher was

excellent at motivating his students in a positive way, and he achieved very good results from

his students with these method. Negative motivation may work with a few student, but many

students work harder and more successfully with some positive reinforcement. Even as a college

student, I still need to receive positive feedback from my instructors. I guess it's just human

nature to want an encouragement and praise.

WRITING TOPICS

Choose one of the topics and write at least one paragraph. Use a variety of articles and other determiners. After you complete your first draft, concentrate on editing your work. Keep in mind the editing practice from this chapter.

1. Using nicknames is a common way for friends and family members to demonstrate friendship or intimacy. What is your nickname or the nickname of someone you know? What does the nickname mean? How did you or this person acquire the nickname? Do you like it? What significance does it have to you, your friends, or family members?

2. Your best friend is currently attending a different school. You would like to convince him or her to transfer to your school. Describe the school you are at now so that your friend will be interested in visiting or even transferring. You may want to describe the beautiful buildings and parks, the excellent faculty, the friendly students, the various social activities, or the interesting surrounding neighborhoods.

Go to page 90 for more practice with articles and other determiners.

CHAPTER 8

Pronouns

PRETEST

Check your understanding of pronouns. Put a check (✓) next to the sentences that are correct.

____ 1. They left the class without you and I.

____ 2. My mother and me took a handwriting analysis class last year.

____ 3. We just got a new puppy, and he is already bigger than your.

____ 4. Victor and Juan practice his pronunciation together.

✓ 5. They are reading by themselves to increase speed.

✓ 6. I left my book at home. May I look at yours?

____ 7. I usually don't like vegetables, but this looks so good.

✓ 8. I loaned someone my notes, but I can't remember where he or she sits.

____ 9. The bicycle trails are fantastic even though there is a lot of pedestrian traffic on it.

✓ 10. Your children can stay with me for the weekend.

EDITING FOCUS

Pronouns, words like *I, him, it, our,* and *themselves* take the place of nouns. They make writing less repetitive and provide links within sentences and between paragraphs. As writer and editor of your writing, make sure that you use pronouns correctly.

> Joanne and Howard bought a new tent. **They** are going camping.
> We sat next to Mr. and Mrs. Jackson. We had an interesting conversation with **them**.
> Grace and I have new shoes. **Mine** are nicer than **hers**.

	Subject Pronouns	Object Pronouns	Possessive Pronouns	Reflexive Pronouns
Singular	I	me	mine	myself
	you	you	yours	yourself
	he	him	his	himself
	she	her	hers	herself
	it	it	its	itself
Plural	we	us	ours	ourselves
	you	you	yours	yourselves
	they	them	theirs	themselves

KINDS OF PRONOUNS

1. Use subject pronouns as the subjects of sentences.

> **You** and **I** should talk more often.
> In the winter, **they** love to ski in Utah.

2. Use object pronouns as the objects of verbs and of prepositions.

> My professor *likes* **me** because I work so hard in her class.
> Mr. Liu gave the package *to* **him**.

3. Use possessive pronouns in place of a possessive adjective + noun.

> John's car is more expensive than **mine**. (*my car*)
> I received my copy in the mail yesterday. Did you receive **yours**? (*your copy*)

NOTE: Don't confuse possessive pronouns with possessive adjectives. A possessive adjective is always used with a noun; a possessive pronoun is always used alone. For more on possessive adjectives, see page 50.

4. Use **reflexive pronouns** instead of object pronouns when the object refers to the same person or thing as the subject.

> *He* always looks at **himself** in the mirror.

> **NOT**
> He always looks at him in the mirror. (him = *another person*)

5. The **demonstrative pronouns** are *this, that, these,* and *those.* They identify or point to nouns. A demonstrative pronoun must agree with the noun it refers to. *This* and *that* refer to singular nouns; *these* and *those* refer to plural nouns.

> He got an A on his history paper. **This** was the best paper he wrote all year.
> Everyone enjoyed the fireworks and dancing. **These** were the highlights of the day.

This and *that* can be used to refer to ideas, situations, and actions that were just mentioned. When you use them in this way, make sure readers know what they refer to.

> The final exam will be difficult. **This** means you will have to study. (This = *the fact that the final will be difficult.*)
> I took three exams last week. **That** was an exhausting experience.

NOTE: Don't confuse demonstrative pronouns with demonstrative adjectives. A demonstrative adjective is always used with a noun; a demonstrative pronoun is always used alone. For more on demonstrative adjectives, see page 50.

6. **Indefinite pronouns** are formed by combining *every, some, any,* and *no* with *one, body,* and *thing* (e.g., *everyone, somebody, anybody, nothing*). Use them to refer to people and things in general or to unspecified people and things.

Use singular verbs for all indefinite pronouns.

> **Everything** *looks* perfect.

Pronouns and possessive adjectives used with indefinite pronouns must also be singular.

> **Everyone** must decide these things for *himself.*

> **OR**

> **Everyone** must decide these things for *himself or herself.*

> **Anyone** can offer *his or her* opinion.

NOTE: See Tip on page 59 for more on *himself* or *herself.*

7. *Another, others,* and *the other(s)* can be used as pronouns. They can also be used as determiners. (See Chapter 7 for more information.)

> If you've finished that book, I'll lend you **another.**
> Some people are here, but we're waiting for **others** to show up.

USING PRONOUNS

1. Choose pronouns carefully. Choose a subject pronoun, object pronoun, or reflexive pronoun as needed in the sentence.

> The car accident seriously injured Michelle and **me**. *(object pronoun for object of the verb)*
>
> NOT
> The car accident seriously injured Michelle and I / myself.

2. Make the pronoun agree with the noun it replaces.

> The *banking industry* is rapidly changing. **It** has to change because of the new technology.
>   (*It* = *banking industry*)
> *Michelle* drives *Gail and me* to school every day. **She** picks **us** up in front of **our** house.
>   (*She* = *Michelle*; *us* and *our* = *Gail and me*)

3. Use pronouns to link your ideas and avoid repetition.

> We asked the counselor to help us with our college applications. **This** resulted in much stronger responses to all the questions on the applications.
>
> NOT
> We asked the counselor to help us with our college applications. Asking the counselor to help us with our college applications resulted in much stronger responses to all the questions on the applications. (without *this*, repetition occurs)

4. Do not use a pronoun if it results in ambiguity—that is, if it is not clear who or what the pronoun refers to.

> If my parents discuss household chores with my brothers, **my brothers** usually get mad.
>
> NOT
> If my parents discuss household chores with my brothers, they usually get mad.
>   (*They* is ambiguous—does it refer to the parents or the brothers?)

5. In some cases a pronoun is meant to refer to either a male or a female. Traditionally, in such cases masculine pronouns *(he, him, his)* have been used. However, it is now common to use *he or she, him or her,* etc.

> Before a *teacher* steps into a classroom, **he** does a lot of preparation. *(traditional)*
> Before a *teacher* steps into a classroom, **he or she** does a lot of preparation.
>   *(now common)*
> Books can be used during the exam, so *each student* should bring **his** on the day of the exam. *(traditional)*
> Books can be used during the exam, so *each student* should bring **his or hers** on the day of the exam. *(now common)*

6. Each clause has one subject. Do not, at a later point in the clause, use a pronoun to repeat the subject.

> **Mr. and Mrs. Anderson, who live in Mexico City, do not like the air quality.**
>
> **OR**
>
> **Mr. and Mrs. Anderson live in Mexico City. They do not like the air quality.**
>
> **NOT**
> Mr. and Mrs. Anderson, who live in Mexico City, they do not like the air quality.

EDITING PRACTICE

1 *Put a check (✓) next to the sentences that use pronouns or possessive adjectives correctly. Correct the sentences that have errors. Be sure to use correct subject-verb agreement if you change a pronoun.*

_____ 1. Ms. Sharpe will discuss the project with Donna and I.

_____ 2. Encouraging someone to smoke when they don't want to is wrong.

_____ 3. My father asked me to do some car repairs, but I couldn't do it right away.

__✓__ 4. The teenagers hurt themselves when they were practicing for the tournament.

_____ 5. Theresa has so much homework that she doesn't have time to do all of them.

__✓__ 6. When a musician gives a concert, he or she must practice before the performance.

_____ 7. Each girl on the basketball team has their strengths.

_____ 8. His parents, who frequently vacation in Hawaii, they love tropical weather.

__✓__ 9. Bob and I just got new shoes. His are larger than mine.

_____ 10. Paul and me are going on vacation.

2 *In the following paragraph, the underlined pronouns are not correct. Write the correct pronoun form above each underlined pronoun. Be sure to use correct subject-verb agreement if you change a pronoun. There may be more than one way to correct some errors.*

The Fourth of July is one of the most popular holidays in the United States. It is the day that Americans celebrate (1) <u>his or her</u> [*their*] independence. Many people no longer think about independence on the Fourth, but others haven't forgotten the real reason for the celebration. A typical Fourth of July includes spending time with family and friends, having picnics, and shooting off fireworks. This is definitely a day that most people don't spend by (2) <u>theirselves</u> [*themselves*]. Many communities celebrate American independence with a pancake breakfast and a parade in the morning. Later in the afternoon, some families have parties in their backyards or at the beach. Barbecues are popular too, because (3) <u>it</u> [*they are*] is casual, and the <u>food,</u> [*Subj.*] which can be hamburgers or hotdogs, (4) <u>it</u> [*they are*] is always good. Once the sun goes down, it's time for fireworks. Even though they are illegal in many places, people still play with (5) <u>it</u> [*them*]. Many communities have professional fireworks so that a <u>child</u> doesn't hurt (6) <u>themselves</u> [*himself*] with (7) <u>it</u> [*the fireworks*]. If an American watches television or listens to the radio on the Fourth, (8) <u>they</u> [*he/she*] will see or hear many patriotic shows to help celebrate the day. Besides all of these festivities, everyone has to wear red, white, and blue or (9) <u>him or her</u> [*he*] looks out of place. These colors are almost mandatory on the Fourth. There are so many holidays to celebrate, but many people consider the Fourth of July to be their favorite holiday compared to (10) <u>another</u> [*others*].

3 *Read the following paragraph. Complete the paragraph with the correct pronoun or possessive adjective.*

Communism is one of the worst economic systems that has ever existed. I know this because my family and _____[*I*]_____ lived under _____[*it*]_____ in Vietnam for many years

1. **I / me / myself**   2. **them / its / it**

during my childhood. This kind of system hurts people because it doesn't provide for

_____[*them*]_____ like it is supposed to. Communism in Vietnam was supposed to

3. **them / theirs / themselves**

establish equality among the people, but _____[*it*]_____ has done almost the opposite, and

4. **we / they / it**

people are now economically segregated just like in the past. The people are supposedly the owners of all the property; however, when I lived in Vietnam, the people didn't control the land by

_____[*themselves*]_____. The result of _____[*this*]_____ is no one has any property and

5. ~~**themselves**~~ / us / ourselves   6. ~~**this**~~ / those / these

all citizens work for the government rather than for _____. A man may

7. himself / theirselves / themselves

work twelve hours a day and still not come home with enough money to support _____

8. his / your / their

family. In addition to economic hardship, people do not have freedom to speak their minds

because the government is afraid _____ might revolt. Each citizen must suppress

9. they / them / their

every thought that _____ has. The Vietnamese cannot even practice religion

10. they / he or she / we

because _____ goes against communist doctrine. In my opinion, communism has

11. these / those / this

turned Vietnam into one of the poorest countries in the world, and _____ laws have

12. our / their / its

turned many Vietnamese citizens against _____their_____ neighbors. Sadly, this is only one tragic

13. its / their / his

result of communism. There are _____.

14. another / others / the other

4   *The following essay has ten errors in the use of pronouns. Find and correct the errors. Be sure to
check for subject-verb agreement if you change a pronoun.*

The Salad Bowl Theory, which describes many societies today, it claims that all immigrants

them

should keep his or her individuality but also add to the dominant culture. This type of society

looks like a salad with many different ingredients that all make up one large dish, but each flavor

is distinct on its own. Many large cities throughout the world are perfect examples of this theory.

They   *themself*

These cities have a number of different ethnic communities that live by itself. However, these

his

communities they also contribute to the overall mix of their cities. Every neighborhood has their

own characteristics, but living together as one large salad helps maintain strong neighborhoods,

cities, states, and countries.

Others feel the Melting Pot Theory describes a better way for different cultures to live

It   *it she*

harmoniously together. This theory states that once an immigrant comes to a new country, they

their

should leave behind the old culture and traditions. In other words, immigrants must "melt" into

the dominant culture. While many immigrant groups in the past have given up his or her culture

them

and language, many groups today fight this theory and try not to lose their.

they are

Although there are other theories, this is two of the most commonly known. It is difficult

to say which theory is more common today. The only thing that can be said accurately is that

itself

immigrants must be comfortable with theirselves and with different cultures in order to survive in

themselves

today's diverse societies.

WRITING TOPICS

Choose one of the topics and write at least one paragraph. Use as many different pronouns as possible. After you complete your first draft, concentrate on editing your work. Keep in mind the editing practice from this chapter.

1. Briefly summarize a movie or book you recently saw or read. Who were the main characters? What did they do? Why did you like or dislike the movie or book? Will you recommend it to your friends? Why or why not?

2. Describe the best teacher you have ever had. What made him or her a good teacher? What are the characteristics of a good teacher? How do good teachers help create better students or people?

Go to page 90 for more practice with pronouns.

CHAPTER 9

Modals

PRE**TEST**

Check your understanding of modals. Put a check (✓) next to the sentences that are correct.

____ 1. Jim should gives his mother a nice gift on Mother's Day.

____ 2. Last semester I had to write three essays in one night because I put them off until the last minute.

____ 3. Mozart was a child prodigy; he can play the piano at a very young age.

____ 4. If you want an A, you can study tonight.

____ 5. This book may be the best one I have ever read.

____ 6. Your mom didn't know where you were, but she said you might be next door.

____ 7. I'm not sure, but I think we are suppose to leave tonight.

____ 8. It snowed so much yesterday that we not able to drive home.

____ 9. Lonnie is so sick that she had better see a doctor soon.

____ 10. I want to offer you a job at my restaurant. I may pay you minimum wage plus tips.

EDITING FOCUS

Modals are auxiliary verbs. They are used with main verbs to give advice and to express ideas like ability, necessity, or possibility. Examples of modals are *can, might,* and *should.* Most modals have more than one meaning. For example, *can* is used for possibility, ability, and permission.

Phrasal modals are expressions with meanings similar to those of modal auxiliaries. They include expressions like *be able to, be supposed to,* and *have to.* As writer and editor of your writing, you need to make sure that you use the correct forms of modals and phrasal modals to express the meaning you want to convey.

FORMING MODALS

PRESENT /FUTURE TIME

1. Modal auxiliaries have only one form. Use a modal + the base form of the verb. The base form of the verb is used with all subjects. Do not add *-s* to the base form for third person singular subjects. For negative statements, put *not* after the modal.

	Affirmative: modal + base form of verb			Negative: modal + not + base form of verb
	can			cannot*
	could			could not
I	will		I	will not
You	would		You	would not
He, She, It	should	+ eat	He, She, It	should not
We	ought to		We	** + eat
You	may		You	may not
They	might		They	might not
	must			must not
	had better			had better not

Cannot is written as one word.
**Americans do not usually use the negative of *ought to.* Use *shouldn't* instead.

He **may need** more time to finish his paper.

NOT
He may needs more time to finish his paper.

He **had better not** drive because there won't be anywhere to park.

NOT
He had not better drive because there won't be anywhere to park.

2. Although modals do not change form with different subjects, phrasal modals with *be* and *have* do change form to agree with the subject.

> **I am supposed to practice today.**
> **Michael has to help his parents move.**
> **John and Kim are able to do the homework.**

3. To make questions and negatives with *have to,* use *do, does, do not,* or *does not.*

> **What do I have to do to get a visa?**
> **Does he have to make an appointment to see her?**
> **I don't have to finish my essay until Friday.**
> **Maria doesn't have to go to class tomorrow.**

PAST TIME

The following are the past tense forms for some modals and phrasal modals.

Present	Past
can	could
have to/has to	had to
am/is/are/able to	was/were able to
am/is/are supposed to	was/were supposed to

> **When I was a child, I could play the violin.**
> **We had to call a tow truck to pull the car out of the ditch.**
> **Their plane wasn't able to take off because of the snowstorm.**
> **We were supposed to call home as soon as we arrived, but we forgot.**

SELF CHECK 1

Correct the errors in modal forms.

1. Financial aid can helps many students continue their education.

2. Desert communities has to start water conservation programs soon.

3. You should study not with the television on.

4. Robert have to prepare to give a presentation.

5. Has Pat to go to the library to do the research?

Meaning	Present	Future	Past
Showing Ability	can am/is/are able to She **can** play the piano very well.	can am/is/are able to	could was/were able to
Making Requests	can could would **Would** you please proofread this essay for me?	can could would will	
Showing Possibility	can may might could I **might** take an art class next semester.	can may might could	
Showing Near Certainty (deduction)	must His office door is locked; he **must** not be here today.	—	
Asking for and Giving Permission	can could may **May** I borrow this book from you? Sure you **can**.	can could may	
Showing Necessity	must has/have to You **must** arrive by 10:15 A.M.	must has/have to	had to
Showing Prohibition	must not cannot You **cannot** talk during the exam.	must not cannot	
Showing Lack of Necessity	do/does not + have to You **do not have to** type the outline for your paper.	do/does not + have to	did not have to
Giving Advice/ Making Suggestions	had better (not) am/is/are supposed to should ought to can could You **should** visit your professor during her office hours for some help.	had better (not) am/is/are supposed to should ought to can could	was supposed to

NOTE: For a comprehensive list of past tense modals, refer to a grammar book.

Correct the errors in modal use.

1. You might not talk to other students during the exam.

2. You had better turn in the essay late or you will fail the course.

3. You must not take a final exam if you don't want to; you can write a research paper instead.

4. Cats may climb trees and see in the dark.

5. The office door is locked and the lights are off; they should be closed today.

TIP

Read your essay out loud several times. Sometimes it's easy to hear grammar errors that your eyes miss during silent reading.

EDITING PRACTICE

1 *Put a check (✓) next to the sentences that use modals correctly. Correct the sentences that have errors.*

____ 1. I know you're busy, so you are not supposed to do the dishes if you don't have time.

____ 2. Diane better pass the test, or she may fail the class.

____ 3. Ava is supposed to turn in her paper a day early.

____ 4. I have a cellular phone, so now he can calls me wherever I go.

____ 5. Can you offer my son a job?

____ 6. You must not ever to call her again.

____ 7. When we first arrived at the airport, we cannot find a place to park.

____ 8. The Nelson family cannot afford to take a vacation this year.

____ 9. John could not come to the game last night because he has to work.

____10. You should not talk on the phone and drive at the same time because it is dangerous.

2 *In the following paragraph, seven of the underlined modal and verb combinations are not correct. Find and correct the errors.*

As we know, we will probably find many differences between schools in a foreign country and schools in the United States. One big difference between Asian and American schools is that in Asian schools the students (1) <u>must stand</u> when the teacher enters the classroom. When I was a student in an Asian school, we (2) <u>have to bow</u> every time a teacher entered. To most Americans, this form of respect (3) <u>must looking</u> strange, and this behavior (4) <u>may seems</u> unusual. Also in my culture, parents and teachers force children to study because they believe the children (5) <u>can not make</u> the decision to study for themselves. Punishment is a common form of motivation in Eastern schools. In my primary school, when we didn't work hard we (6) <u>were supposed to receive</u> a painful slap on the hand. At that time punishment was normal to me, and I think it probably gave me the discipline to work hard in school. When my family and I came to the United States, we (7) <u>has to adapt</u> to a very different educational style. It is still hard for me to believe that physical punishment is illegal in American schools. Now I enjoy the fact that I (8) <u>would learn</u> my lessons on my own and not because a teacher or parent is forcing me. After being educated in two countries, I would like my children to receive a combination of both educational styles. I hope they (9) <u>must see</u> the benefits from the educational traditions of both cultures.

3 *Underline the modals in the following sentences. In your own words, write the meaning of each sentence in the blank. Use a modal different from the one in the sentence to express the meaning, or give the meaning without using a modal.*

Example: You <u>have to</u> put the stamp in the upper right-hand corner of the envelope.

Meaning: <u>It is necessary to put the stamp in the upper right-hand corner of the envelope.</u>

1. Arman, Isabel, and Ali may go out for dinner tonight.

   Meaning: _____

2. In class today, my instructor said we have to read the whole textbook this quarter.

   Meaning: _____

3. I should learn to speak a second language, but I do not have much free time.

   Meaning: _____

4. Tourists can eat a lot of delicious food on a vacation in Italy.

   Meaning: _____

5. Marcus must learn how to swim before he takes the scuba diving class.

   Meaning: _____

4 *Underline the ten modal and verb combinations used in this essay. Six have errors. Find and correct the errors. There may be more than one way to correct some errors.*

In the novel *Black Boy,* by Richard Wright, the author writes about his own life. Throughout the novel Richard Wright is a very independent person. This may be because Richard's father leaves the family when Richard is still a boy. Therefore, Richard is able to be responsible for doing the household chores and taking care of his younger brother. Richard also have to stand up for himself, which is often difficult for a child. Even though he experiences hardship as a child, Richard is able to maintain his curiosity and interest in life. Later, more unhappiness comes to Richard and his family. His mother has a stroke and is partially paralyzed. Richard is forced to take help from the neighbors. Soon after, Richard's grandmother comes to help the family. She must look after Richard's mother and brother better than Richard can. Later, other relatives arrive and decide that Grandmother is able not to watch Richard's family any longer. After his grandmother leaves, Richard has to live with his Uncle Edward, and Richard's brother goes to live with his Aunt Maggie.

I liked reading this novel about Richard Wright and how he reacts to racial issues in America. The story may helps readers understand issues that African Americans face in the United States. I prefer learning history through a novel like *Black Boy* to learning through history books. Studying books like *Black Boy* might encourage students to explore complex issues with interest and passion. I can not forget the lessons I learned about racism and hardship from this novel.

WRITING TOPICS

Choose one of the topics and write at least one paragraph. Use a variety of modals. After you complete your first draft, concentrate on editing your work. Keep in mind the editing practice from this chapter.

1. What should or must each of us do to make the world a better and safer place to live? What could each of us do to help reduce problems like racism, pollution, or violence?

2. The norms that children must follow are different from the ones adults must follow. What are some rules that children must follow, and what are others that adults have to follow? What could you do as a child that you are not allowed to do now? What can you do now that you were not supposed to do as a child?

Go to page 91 for more practice with modals.

CHAPTER 10

Verb Forms, Gerunds, and Infinitives

PRETEST

Check your understanding of verb forms, gerunds, and infinitives. Put a check (✓) next to the sentences that are correct.

____ 1. Jun didn't took the driver's test.

____ 2. I haven't boughten any new CDs in a month.

____ 3. The teacher let us reviewed our partner's first draft of the essay.

____ 4. Are you interested in going to the play-off game this weekend?

____ 5. They avoid to drive at rush hour.

____ 6. Emily loves to read nineteenth-century English literature.

____ 7. Please don't make me to practice anymore.

____ 8. Johnnie is accustomed to studying late at night.

____ 9. Mr. Tang plans to go on a cruise to Cuba from Mexico.

____ 10. I miss to see my family.

EDITING FOCUS

VERB FORMS

There are five basic verb forms in English:

Base form	write
Third person singular	writes
Simple past	wrote
Present participle (*-ing* form)	writing
Past participle (*-ed/-en/-t* form)	written

Although these verb forms have been discussed in earlier chapters, this chapter will review the rules for using them. If the verb form in a particular sentence is not correct, the sentence is ungrammatical. As writer and editor of your writing, you need to make sure that you choose the correct verb forms.

THE SIMPLE TENSES

1. In the simple present, use the base form and the third person singular. Use the auxiliary verb *do* in negatives and questions except with the verb *be*. (See Chapter 1.)

> I usually **make** dinner.   He sometimes **makes** dinner.
> John **does not like** to eat red meat.   Where **do** they **eat** lunch?

2. In the simple past, use the simple past form of the verb. Use the auxiliary verb *did* in negatives and questions except with the verb *be*. (See Chapter 2.)

> My cousin **visited** me last month.   We **went** to many places together.
> They **didn't have** time to see us.   Where **did** Rich and Darla **go**?

NOTE: The auxiliary *do* is always followed by the base form of the verb.

> They **didn't come**.

THE PROGRESSIVE TENSES

In the present progressive and past progressive, use the auxiliary *be* followed by the present participle of the main verb. The form of *be* shows present or past time. (See Chapters 1 and 2.)

> **Are** you **doing** your homework now? *(present progressive)*
> Last year at this time, I **was visiting** friends in Brazil. *(past progressive)*

THE PERFECT TENSES

In the present perfect and past perfect, use the auxiliary *have* followed by the past participle of the main verb. The form of *have* shows present or past time. (See Chapters 1 and 2.)

> **Has** she **seen** the new Russian film yet? *(present perfect)*
> The Halloween party **had ended** by midnight. *(past perfect)*

Remember to check a dictionary to make sure you are using the correct forms for irregular simple past verbs and past participles.

MODALS

In sentences about the present or future, modals are always followed by the base form of the main verb. (See Chapter 9.)

I should write a thank-you note to the hosts.
Will you **come** with us next week?

SELF CHECK 1

Correct the errors involving verb forms.

1. Did Bill Clinton won the election in 1996?

2. Melissa and Carson don't be in school today.

3. The kitten that lives next door visiting us right now.

4. I just bought a new dress. You buy one too?

5. She can plays the piano very well.

GERUNDS AND INFINITIVES

In addition to the five basic forms, verbs in English also have a gerund form (verb + *-ing*) and an infinitive form (*to* + verb). In these forms, however, the verb no longer acts as a verb. Gerunds and infinitives act as nouns—either as subjects, as objects of verbs and prepositions, or as complements.

VERB + GERUND OR INFINITIVE

Some verbs can take either gerunds or infinitives as their objects. These verbs include the following:

begin   continue   hate   like   love   prefer   start

She hates *swimming / to swim* in the ocean.
They've loved *reading / to read* since they were children.
We preferred *studying / to study* on the fourth floor of the library last year.

VERB + GERUND

Some verbs can take gerunds but not infinitives as their objects. These verbs include the following:

appreciate	delay	dislike	finish	mention	miss	suggest
avoid	discuss	enjoy	keep	mind	quit	

I avoid *working out* at the gym.
Aaron dislikes *traveling* by bus.
Susan suggested *seeing* the new ballet at Lincoln Center.

VERB + INFINITIVE

Some verbs take an infinitive or a noun + infinitive, but cannot take a gerund as their object. These verbs include the following:

advise	encourage	intend	order	seem
agree	expect	invite	plan	tell
ask	force	learn	pretend	want
decide	hope	offer	remind	warn

Susan agreed *to go* with him to a concert.
The university requires potential students *to write* an essay.

TIP

If you are unsure whether a verb is followed by an infinitive or a gerund, a grammar book can give you this information.

PREPOSITION + GERUND

- Prepositions such as *in, on, by, for, with,* etc., can be followed by gerunds but not infinitives.

  He made up an excuse for *arriving* late to dinner.

- Two-word verbs and other verb + preposition combinations can also be followed by gerunds but not infinitives.

  I often put off *studying* until right before a test.
  I am accustomed to *studying* until 1:00 A.M.
  Have you thought about *going* to graduate school?

Common two-word verbs followed by gerunds include:

give up	insist on	keep on	put off

Other common verb + preposition combinations followed by gerunds include:

apologize for	complain about	look forward to	prohibit (someone) from	talk about
believe in	insist on	plan on	take care of	think about

Common *be* + adjective + preposition combinations followed by gerunds include:

be accustomed to	be excited about	be preoccupied with	be worried about
be bored with	be interested in	be tired of	

TIP

Be careful! Do not confuse the preposition *to* (in *be accustomed to, look forward to,* etc.) with the *to* used in the infinitive (*to go, to be,* etc.). The preposition *to* is followed by a gerund. The infinitive *to* is followed by the base form of the verb.

VERB + BASE FORM

The verbs *make, have, let,* and *help* can all be used to write about causing someone to do something or making it possible for someone to do something. Used this way, these words are followed by a noun phrase or pronoun + the base form of a verb. *Help* can be followed by an infinitive instead of a base form.

> The coach **made us** *run* another lap, and then he **had us** *do* more push-ups.
> She **lets her daughter** *go out* on dates.
> **Can you help me** *(to) paint* the house?

SELF CHECK 2

Correct the errors involving verbs with gerunds, infinitives, or base forms.

1. Healthy eaters dislike to eat a lot of sugar.

2. He hopes to seeing a Broadway show in New York.

3. The hike made them felt tired all day.

4. They are excited about join the club.

5. I look forward to swim in the lake this summer.

> **TIP**
>
> Edit your writing on a printed copy rather than on the computer screen. Editing is much more thorough and accurate on paper.

EDITING PRACTICE

1 *Put a check (✓) next to the sentences that use verb forms, gerunds, and infinitives correctly. Correct the sentences that have errors.*

____ 1. The counselor advised us to begin the university application process early.

____ 2. Negligent pet owners let their animals to wander the streets.

____ 3. Mr. Gong made his son play the violin.

____ 4. Some people believe criticism helps children behaving appropriately.

____ 5. The Berlin Wall doesn't divides East and West Germany anymore.

____ 6. Mrs. Hasam suggested taking a charter flight because it was less expensive.

____ 7. I love the sound when the wind is blow through the trees.

____ 8. The San Francisco campus cover three hundred acres of land.

____ 9. Has the principal being to your house?

_____ 10. I apologized for losing Anthony's book.

_____ 11. I didn't found the ring I lost last week.

_____ 12. The students look forward to finish the project.

2 *In the following paragraph, the underlined verbs are not correct. Write the correct verb form above each underlined verb phrase.*

For many people, personal health and healthcare are important parts of their lives. A common way to deal with health issues is through diet and exercise. On average, the typical person (1) is live longer than in the past but not necessarily in a healthier way. Many people (2) dislike to make lifestyle changes even though the changes (3) may making them feel better in old age. People (4) do not likes to sacrifice now for uncertain benefits in the future. However, if problems such as obesity and high blood pressure are not controlled, a majority of sufferers (5) will developing heart disease in the future. More women than men exercise regularly and (6) have improve their eating habits. However, there are probably few differences between men's and women's health. The main difference is between people who (7) decide eating a healthy, well-balanced diet and those who (8) let themselves to become lazy when it comes to food. This goes for exercise as well. Even though the number one health concern for most people is weight, and many (9) are preoccupied with lose weight, obesity rates continue to rise. A healthy diet makes one (10) enjoy to exercise more, and a moderate amount of exercise (11) helps people eating well. Therefore, both are necessary for maintaining a healthy lifestyle. It's ironic that in the past people (12) did not worried as much as we do today about living healthy lives, yet their health was probably better than ours.

3 *Read the following paragraph. Complete the paragraph with the correct form of each verb given.*

In the United States during World War II, many Japanese Americans were sent to internment camps.[1] These Americans did not _____ why they were being treated as
                                                              1. understand
criminals; however, the U.S. government believed that Japanese Americans might _____
                                                                                    2. give
American secrets to Japan. Many Japanese Americans were sent to a camp called Manzanar.

Government and camp officials did not _____ the camp residents _____
                                                          3. help   **4. adapt**
to their new surroundings. The Japanese Americans were on their own and could only

_____ for an improved situation. As the U.S. involvement in World War II was
      5. hope

_____, the government let the internees² _____ to U.S. locations farther east.
      6. end   **7. move**
After the war had finally _____, Japanese Americans were forced _____ the
                                          8. end   **9. leave**
camps. They began _____ about resuming their shattered lives. Over the past decades,
                               10. think
other Americans have slowly been learning more about this episode in U.S. history and are

interested in _____ to correct past wrongs. Thinking about past injustices reminds
                          11. try
us _____ these kinds of actions before they happen again.
      12. prevent

> ¹**internment camps:** areas where prisoners are held, especially during war
> ²**internees:** people in internment camps, prisoners

4 *The following paragraph has ten errors in the use of verb forms, gerunds, and infinitives. Find and correct the errors.*

Los Angeles is a city that is full of excitement and diversity. It is unfortunate that the city has receive a lot of bad press because of the smog, the crime, and the riots in the early 1990s. Although some negative perceptions of Los Angeles may be accurate, tourists should not to overlook the city when they make their travel plans. In fact, southern California residents ought to think about visit downtown more often. This area has becomes a center of excitement and diversity. Koreatown, Little Tokyo, and Olvera Street all exist within several square miles of each other. This racial diversity helps Angelenos understanding other cultures and beliefs and in addition, helps them accepting differences more easily. The city's art community is also first-rate. Previously, Los Angeles did not had a theater district like New York City does, but now there are several theater complexes and many small theaters throughout the city. The one thing Los Angeles has always being famous for is Hollywood, and it's better than ever. Hollywood is responsible for entertain the world and, like the rest of the city, promises to impressing visitors and residents alike.

WRITING TOPICS

Choose one of the topics and write at least one paragraph. Use a variety of verbs from the lists given in this chapter as well as some of your own. After you complete your first draft, concentrate on editing your work. Keep in mind the editing practice from this chapter.

1. Everyone has different ways of spending his or her free time. Write about one or more ways that you like to spend your leisure time. Do you exercise, read, play sports, shop, sleep, or study? How often do you do this? Is this an activity that you do alone or with a group? How does the activity help you relax, clear your mind, or feel better?

2. Some people prefer to live downtown in large cities, others prefer the suburbs, and many like the countryside. Which do you prefer and why? These places are different from one another in terms of pace of life, safety, recreational opportunities, education, and job options. What aspects do you like about one location? What do you dislike about others? Tell where you live now and where you have lived in the past. How have these locations helped you develop your preferences?

Go to page 91 for more practice with verb forms, gerunds, and infinitives.

CHAPTER 11

Word Forms

PRE**TEST**

Check your understanding of word forms. Put a check (✓) next to the sentences that are correct.

_____ 1. E-mail is the greatest form of communication.

_____ 2. The movie was so scared.

_____ 3. My best friend finished the work very quick.

_____ 4. Right now Dan is the worst swimmer in the class, but he tries very hard.

_____ 5. We past many large animals along the road in northern Canada.

_____ 6. Greg is the most fast reader in the class.

_____ 7. The class was pleased with the high test scores.

_____ 8. I finished the entirely book in one night.

_____ 9. You have to get permissioned to use the color copier in the library.

_____ 10. Erica and Ray are working harder than they did last year.

EDITING FOCUS

Words belong to different parts of speech. That is, they are nouns, verbs, adjectives, adverbs, prepositions, and so on. The form of a word changes according to its part of speech. For a sentence to be grammatical, correct word forms must be used. Consider the related word forms in the following sentences:

Verb	Reading **has strengthened** Jeong's vocabulary.
Noun	Politics is one of Jeong's **strengths**.
Adjective	Jeong is a **strong** public speaker.
Adverb	Jeong spoke **strongly** in favor of the new president.

SUFFIXES

The suffix, or ending, of a word can help you recognize the part of speech. When you write and edit, make sure you use the correct suffixes. (For example, *-ent* is an adjective suffix, and *-ence* is a noun suffix.)

Joon is an intellig**ent** student.

NOT

Joon is an intelligence student.

Independ**ence** is an important value.

NOT

Independent is an important value.

> **TIP**
>
> In addition to the lists below, use a dictionary if you are unsure of suffixes. Many dictionaries include suffixes, indicating what parts of speech they go with and what their general meanings are.

VERB SUFFIXES

Here are four common verb suffixes:

-ate	investi**ate**	-ify	noti**fy**
-en	broad**en**	-ize	hospital**ize**

NOUN SUFFIXES

Here are some common noun suffixes:

-ment	involve**ment**	-er	writ**er**
-ness	happi**ness**	-or	act**or**
-ion	permiss**ion**	-ism	commun**ism**
-ity	possibil**ity**	-ist	social**ist**
-ance	toler**ance**	-ship	friend**ship**
-ence	refer**ence**	-cy	accura**cy**

ADVERB SUFFIX

Adverbs have only one common suffix:

-ly   happily

ADJECTIVE SUFFIXES

Here are some common adjective suffixes:

-ous	famous	-ing	boring
-ful	helpful	-ed	excited
-less	careless	-ish	foolish
-ive	creative	-ate	literate
-able	acceptable	-y	scary
-ible	responsible	-ly	friendly
-ant	tolerant	-like	childlike
-ent	dependent	-some	handsome
-ic	allergic	-an/-ian	African, Floridian
-al	classical	-ese	Chinese

The adjective suffix -ing means "causing a feeling." The adjective suffix -ed means "experiencing a feeling." For example, an *exciting* person causes a feeling of excitement in other people; an *excited* person feels excitement. The -ed adjectives are often used to describe people, whereas the -ing adjectives are often used to describe things and actions as well as people.

He was a *boring* teacher, so there were many *bored* students in his class.
At the end of the *tiring* day, the *tired* children were happy to go home.

SELF CHECK 1

Correct the errors involving suffixes.

1. I am interesting in Arab literature.

2. Read the chapter careful.

3. Is she a success businesswoman?

4. I am disappoint about my math grade.

5. Check in the back of the book for a referencing.

COMPARATIVES AND SUPERLATIVES

COMPARATIVES OF ADJECTIVES AND ADVERBS

Use comparatives when you are comparing two things.

1. Add the comparative suffix -er to one-syllable adjectives and adverbs. Since -er means "more (than)," do not use *more* with a word that has an -er suffix.

Marvin is **busier** than I am. *(adjective)*   Ali works **harder** than Tim. *(adverb)*

NOT   NOT

Marvin is more busier than I am.   Ali works more harder than Tim.

2. With most adjectives and adverbs of two syllables or more, use *more* for comparatives.

> **I am serious about work, but Marvin is more serious.** *(adjective)*
> **I work carefully, but he works more carefully.** *(adverb)*

3. Some adjectives and adverbs have irregular comparative forms.

Better is the comparative form of the adjective *good* and the adverb *well.*

Jose is a good socializer.	**Jose is a better socializer than Lee.** *(adjective)*
Marie sings well.	**Marie sings better than Paula.** *(adverb)*

Worse is the comparative form of the adjective *bad* and the adverb *badly.*

My spelling is bad.	**My spelling is worse than yours.** *(adjective)*
Martin drives badly.	**Martin drives worse than Chris.** *(adverb)*

TIP

Be careful! *Good* **is an adjective, and** *well* **is an adverb. Do not use** *good* **as an adverb.**

He speaks Italian very well.

NOT
He speaks Italian very good.

---

4. Use *-less* with all adjectives and adverbs in making comparisons.

> **I'm less busy than Marvin** *(is).*
> **I work less carefully than Marvin** *(does).*

NOTE: If you mention the second thing being compared, include *than.* You may also include the verb or its auxiliary.

> **I am** *taller* **than my sisters** *(are).*
> **I walk** *faster* **than you** *(do).*

SUPERLATIVES OF ADJECTIVES AND ADVERBS

Use superlatives when you are comparing three or more things.

1. Add the superlative suffix *-est* to one-syllable adjectives and adverbs. Include *the* before the adjective or adverb. Since *-est* means "the most," do not use *the most* with a word that has an *-est* suffix.

Alyssa is the tallest in the class. *(adjective)*	**Cathy reads the fastest in the class.** *(adverb)*
NOT	**NOT**
Alyssa is the most tallest in the class.	**Cathy reads the most fastest in the class.**

2. With most adjectives and adverbs of two syllables or more, use *the most*.

> Several stores are convenient, but this one is really **the most convenient**.
> I prefer this train to the others, because it runs **the most frequently**.

3. Some adjectives and adverbs have irregular superlative forms.

Best is the superlative form of the adjective *good* and the adverb *well*.

> Her university has a good education department, but this university has **the best** education department. *(adjective)*
> I write well, but you write **the best** in our study group. *(adverb)*

Worst is the superlative form of the adjective *bad* and the adverb *badly*.

> No one in my family is a good singer, and I'm **the worst** of all. *(adjective)*
> She performed the **worst** she has performed all year. *(adverb)*

4. Use *the least* with all adjectives and adverbs.

> This is **the least busy** time of the year for the store. *(adjective)*
> This engine runs **the least efficiently** of the three. *(adverb)*

5. The superlative adjective or adverb is often followed by a noun and/or a prepositional phrase, which indicates what is being compared.

> Angelica is **the most popular** *girl in the class*.
> Joseph works **the hardest** *in the class*.

TIP

Remember: an adjective describes a noun or pronoun, and an adverb describes a verb, an adjective, or another adverb.

SELF CHECK 2

Correct the errors involving comparatives and superlatives.

1. He has the expensivest stereo.

2. A Honda is more cheaper than a Mercedes-Benz.

3. We have the baddest record in the league.

4. Is the highway convenienter than the side streets?

5. I did very good on my biology exam.

EASILY CONFUSED WORDS

The following words sound similar or the same and are easily confused in writing. The words are often different parts of speech, so think carefully when you use them.

accept	= verb	The school accepted him for next term.
except	= preposition	We saw all of the movie except for the first five minutes.
affect	= verb	The weather affects our moods.
effect	= noun	The research is about the effect of sunlight on people's moods.
its	= possessive adjective	My plant has outgrown its pot.
it's	= it is	I'm not sure where my key is, but I think it's in the car.
lose	= verb	Clara is always losing her car keys.
loose	= adjective	These pants are loose around the waist.
loss	= noun	The soccer team has three wins and two losses.
lost	= verb (past tense)	I lost my credit cards last weekend.
	= adjective	The lost child is wandering the street.
past	= noun	My grandmother lives in the past.
	= adjective	This past year has been difficult.
	= preposition	He walked past me without stopping.
passed	= verb (past tense)	Nicole passed the test.
pass	= verb (present tense)	I hope we pass the final.
than	= function word	That restaurant has better pizza than pasta.
then	= adverb	We're going to dinner and then to a movie.
there	= function word	There are many models of computers to choose from.
	= adverb	Look over there!
their	= possessive adjective	Did you get their letter?
they're	= they are	They're going to be late today.
to	= preposition	Jason can walk to the store.
too	= adverb	It's too early for dinner.
two	= number	I've got two tickets for the game tonight.
whose	= possessive adjective	We're not sure whose book that is.
who's	= who is	That's the woman who's moving in next door.
worse	= comparative form of bad and badly	Robin is worse than I am at bowling.
worst	= superlative form of bad and badly	Which flavor is the worst?
your	= possessive adjective	Have you done your homework?
you're	= you are	You think you're so funny.

Correct the errors involving easily confused words.

1. Do you have there phone number?

2. I did to much work last night.

3. My broken toe effects my posture.

4. I know where your going.

5. We past the airport on our way home.

> **TIP**
>
> Use the spell-check tool on your computer before you print your paper. It will help you catch general spelling errors. Be careful, however, because it won't find errors in easily confused words.

EDITING PRACTICE

1 *Put a check (✓) next to the sentences that use word forms correctly. Correct the sentences that have errors. If necessary, use a dictionary to check for the correct word form.*

____ 1. This city and university campus are diversity.

____ 2. I feel embarrass when I receive a poor grade on an exam.

____ 3. You should notify your teacher if you are going to be absent.

____ 4. Which way is the easiest?

____ 5. Responsible is something you learn as you become an adult.

____ 6. He has a distance friend that is coming to visit next month.

____ 7. The computer industry is stronger than the manufacturing industry.

____ 8. Phong had feelings of happy, doubt, and pain.

____ 9. I'm not going to sacrifice friends and family to become more richer.

____ 10. She doesn't accept your answer.

____ 11. They dance so good together.

____ 12. That is the importantest paper that I have ever signed.

2 *In the following essay, the underlined words are not correct. Write the correct word above each underlined error. Use a dictionary if necessary to check for the correct word form.*

The novel *Travels with Charley* describes the America that John Steinbeck discovers as he travels from one (1) <u>coastal</u> to the other. He is traveling alone (2) <u>accept</u> for a companion named Charley, a big (3) <u>friend</u> dog. We get to know Charley (4) <u>good</u> by the end of the book because the author spends so much time with him. Even though Charley is lazy, he is (5) <u>more smart</u> than other dogs. And in some cases Steinbeck is even (6) <u>foolisher</u> than Charley. Charley is a trustworthy dog. He also adds (7) <u>excited</u> moments to the story. In fact, what Charley does when Steinbeck is stopped by the Canadian police is one of the (8) <u>interestingest</u> parts of the novel.

Even with (9) <u>it's</u> good parts, we were (10) <u>disappointing</u> in *Travels with Charley*. We both expected to read more about North American life (11) <u>then</u> Charley's adventures. The (12) <u>pleasantest</u> part of the book is when Steinbeck writes about the North American scenery and people. The book also does a good job of showing how people need supportive friendship, even if it's only a dog that provides it.

3 Read the following paragraph. Complete the paragraph with the correct form of each word given. If necessary, use a dictionary to select suffixes for different parts of speech.

The traditional roles that men and women have played throughout history have been very

_____. In many _____ , the majority of jobs and activities are still divided
    1. differ   2. culture

into men's or women's work, although this practice is changing. In _____ cultures
             3. tradition

or families, the women accept the subservient role and are _____ on men for
             4. depend

_____ support and leadership within the family. In many parts of the world, these
  5. finance

roles are changing as women take over some of the duties that men have _____ held.
             6. tradition

In many cases men _____ hand over their positions of dominance. Men and women
        7. glad

now have equal educational opportunities and job prospects after their _____ from
             8. graduate

high school or college. It is impossible to say which system is the _____ one, but
             9. good

people no longer question a woman's right to pursue a career and have a family or a man's

_____ to make the family his first priority. These are _____ advances for
  10. decide   11. signify

both sexes and changes that make life _____ than it was in the past.
           12. easy

4 *The following paragraph has ten errors in the use of word forms and easily confused words. Find and correct the errors. If necessary, use a dictionary to find the correct word form.*

When I am asked to describe myself as a writer, I have a difficult time writing down my thoughts. I am a slowly writer and find the most tough part of an essay to write is the introduction. Sometimes I sit impatient in front of the computer for hours with only a few words to show for my time. I know writing is a slow process, but I am frustrating a lot of the time. Once I am passed the introduction, I write the body and conclusion more rapid. In fact, to be honest, I almost enjoy writing by the time I finish a paper. It's a big accomplishment, and I always feel proud of myself. In-class writing can be an even bigger problem than out-of-class writing. An essay exam is always frightened, especially when I'm given only a short period of time to complete it. I usually write very slow on these tests and never have time to finish. Even though writing makes me feel uncomfortable, I know I have to work on this importance skill. I definitely plan on becoming a good writer as quickly as possible. My teachers keep telling me that if I write oftener, I'll be more comfortable and less anxious about putting my thoughts on paper.

WRITING TOPICS

Choose one of the topics and write at least one paragraph. After you complete your first draft, concentrate on editing your work. Keep in mind the editing practice from this chapter.

1. Many people believe that in Western societies or countries the elderly are not treated well. From your experiences or observations, is this true? Compare how the elderly are treated in two cultures that you are familiar with.

2. People own pets for companionship, protection, or any number of other reasons. Do you have a pet now, or did you have one in the past? Why or why not? Why do people like pets? Do you plan on having a pet in the future? Why or why not? Which type of animal makes the best pet?

Go to page 91 for more practice with word forms.

CHAPTER 12

Extra Editing Practice

Use the following pieces of writing to practice editing for grammar points that you have focused on in the previous chapters.

When you edit your own writing, it is important to look for a variety of grammatical errors; therefore, the exercises in this chapter require that you edit for more than one type of grammatical structure.

TIP

Read your essay many times. You will find your errors more easily if you check for only one grammatical point at a time.

PRESENT TIME TENSES AND SUBJECT-VERB AGREEMENT

1 *Edit carefully for verb errors in the present time tenses and in subject-verb agreement. There are ten errors in the following paragraph.*

After most students graduate from college, they have found nice jobs and begin earning money. However, few people take the time to investigate nontraditional opportunities that are available in nonprofit, public service, and government organizations. This seems to be a path that more recent graduates are currently exploring. Over the past decade, students has had the chance to choose from many types of employers and select the opportunity that are the most beneficial for each of them. Sometimes this may not be the job that pays the most money. Many times, the knowledge that a new graduate gains in a low-paying or nontraditional position are more valuable for his or her future. Spending two or three years in the Peace Corps or Teach America help students learn about themselves and about the world around them. The monetary sacrifices a recent graduate make will hopefully be rewarded in future positions. In addition to future job benefits, the friends and experiences that a person gains in less conventional positions are worth more than money. In other words, many of the sacrifices graduates makes early in their careers will be fully rewarded later on. Volunteerism is being another way to gain important job training and experience. New opportunities are coming from the most unexpected places, and many times volunteer work is that unexpected place. These kinds of opportunities present themselves throughout life, but the time to begin looking for them are now.

PAST TIME TENSES AND SUBJECT-VERB AGREEMENT

2 *Edit carefully for verb errors in the past time tenses and in subject-verb agreement. There are ten errors in the following essay.*

I had always wanted to study and learn more about rain forests, and my opportunity was finally arriving when a group of biology and botany students from all over the world organized a working holiday in Central America. I had signed up right away.

The location that we were living and studying in were one of the best places in Central America to observe the wonders of the rain forest. On the first day, I saw the biodiversity that the rain forest was containing. During the two months we were being there, we saw plants and animals that I never knowed existed. I think the diversity of life were incredible to even the most experienced students. Some of us had the rare opportunity to observe a plant that we have never seen before. Studying in this environment with amazing plants and animals was the best experience of my life.

When I return from the rain forest, I was even more committed to preserving our environment. I had recommended this kind of working holiday to all my fellow students. Even today I feel that this is an experience people from all fields should have in order to truly appreciate the world that we are living in and the delicate state it is in.

TIME SHIFTS AND FUTURE TIME

3 *Edit carefully for errors in time shifts and future time. There are twelve errors in the following paragraph.*

Why didn't I stop them? Why didn't I call the police? Why didn't I do anything at all? In horror, I turned back and look at the bleeding man on the floor of the convenience store as the thieves were rushing out the door. I faced my cowardice and had felt such agony. I experienced a lot of guilt for not acting. Shame rushed through my entire mind and body. Even though I have a cellular phone at the time, I never thought to call the police—all because I was scared. Until that moment, I always believe I was a tough person, someone who stood up for justice. However, at that instant, I saw a side of myself that I am still not proud of. Since that shameful day, I have often thought about that moment. In general, I know that fear caused people to behave in unexpected ways. Before that day, I thought I was above that. However, I was wrong. I hoped that in the future, I will react differently. I try to be more brave. Hopefully, I never experience something that horrible again. However, if I do, I am going do the right thing. I now know that the shame I feel today is worse than the fear I feel on that day. Those few seconds teach me the importance of standing up for what I believe in rather than just talking about those beliefs. This is a lesson that I think changes my future behavior.

COUNT AND NONCOUNT NOUNS; ARTICLES AND OTHER DETERMINERS

4 *Edit carefully for errors in count and noncount nouns as well as articles and other determiners. There are ten errors in the following paragraph.*

It was a cold night in the middle of winter, but the bright streetlights and yellow stars made the chilly, 35-degrees night seem a little warmer. It wasn't cold enough to snow, although a white covering of snows would have added to the winter scene. I was driving my bright red car, passing one houses after another. I imagined the people behind each front doors enjoying family gathering and a nice dinner. All I felt was emptiness and absolute lonelinesses. My usual positive outlook was not able to melt the frosty feeling inside of me. I shook my head, trying to stop all the sad thoughts. Thinking too much wasn't going to help the situation anyway. I chose to give up the struggle going on inside my head and concentrate only on driving along the empty road. The significances of a moment was not clear to me at time. All of that would become apparent in the next few hour.

PRONOUNS; DEMONSTRATIVE AND POSSESSIVE ADJECTIVES

5 *Edit carefully for errors in pronouns and demonstrative and possessive adjectives. There are nine errors in the following paragraph.*

I learned an important lesson about friendship when I was fourteen years old. My family and me were living in a town that was out in the country. It was a small sleepy town whose school didn't offer many after-school activities other than playing basketball and just hanging out. I thought I was pretty good at both activities and did it whenever I could. I used to play basketball every day after school, after hanging out with my friends. Even though I played with him almost every day, they didn't think I was good enough to join his competitive team. I noticed that all the competitive players in my town wore NBA basketball jerseys. I really wanted to join that team and thought that if I wore one, I would be allowed to join. My parents finally bought me two different team jerseys, and I was so happy with this jerseys. It was a very sad day for myself when I wore a jersey and still wasn't asked to join the team. Later, it became clear that the team members were never interested in myself. Not long after this, my family moved away, and I made new friends in ours new town, but I'll never forget the lesson that I learned about friendship. True friends help his friends in all situations, not just when it's convenient.

MODALS; VERB FORMS; GERUNDS AND INFINITIVES

6 *Edit carefully for errors in modals, verb forms, and gerunds and infinitives. There are ten errors in the following paragraph. There may be more than one way to correct some errors.*

Peer pressure has being a common problem for many high school students over the past several decades. Many teenagers feel they might not say no to their friends because acceptance is very important at this time in their lives. Sometimes peer pressure can be positive and other times it can be negative. A lot of adolescents make their friends to begin smoking, drinking, cutting school, and driving too fast. In contrast, a student may decides to study, play sports, and joining clubs because of positive peer pressure. During the transition from junior high to high school, I saw the best student change to the worst student due to the bad influences of his peers. As a young adult, I now enjoy to think about the many good influences in high school that helped me continuing my education. Because I was fortunate to have positive role models during my teenage years, in my future career I plan help teenagers who are facing many negative influences and are thinking about give in to peer pressure. If a teenager has one positive role model, it has to mean the difference between success and failure.

WORD FORMS; COMPARATIVES AND SUPERLATIVES; EASILY CONFUSED WORDS

7 *Edit carefully for errors in word forms, comparatives and superlatives, and easily confused words. There are twelve errors in the following paragraph.*

It was a day like any other as Kellie and I started peddling away from school on our bike ride home. It was the most hot afternoon of the spring, and we anticipation spending it by Kellie's swimming pool. We had a lot of bored homework, but that could wait until we had worked on our tans for a few hours. After we had unlocked our bikes, Kellie rode away a little more fast than I did. I followed her as she wove her way through the basketball and volleyball courts just as some of the teams were beginning to practice. As we approached a narrow passage between the tennis courts and the gym, we thought the way looked clearly, and we turned the corner. To our surprising, the football players had just begun to make there way through the passage. This gave us barely enough room to maneuver ourselves and our bikes passed them. The passage was to narrow for us to turn around, so we were forced to make our way slow down the path with the football players coming toward us. Because there were no adults, some of these athletes grabbed our backpacks and made unkind remarks. At that moment I knew the true meaning of helplessness. The moment made Kellie and me feel frighten, but we sure learned to ride our bikes quick!

CHAPTER 1 Present Time Tenses

Read the following selection from the Newport Beach Light *newspaper. Choose the correct form of the verb.*

Triple Threat

Jillianne Whitfield _____ to play basketball, [play] soccer and run track. But her real
           1. loves / is loving

passion is on the diamond,[1] and it isn't the softball diamond. It's playing baseball with the boys.

   "There's no action in softball. It's too slow for me," said Jillianne. "I _____
                                          2. have played / play

baseball since I was in first grade."

   When the 12-year-old multitalented athlete isn't kicking soccer balls and dribbling

basketballs, she _____ the aluminum bat and chattering with teammates.
       3. is swinging / has swung
   "I got started playing hardball because I wanted to give it a try," said Jillianne. "I loved

playing my first year and I _____ playing since."
       4. am not stopping / haven't stopped
   While Jillianne waits for the baseball season to start, she keeps busy playing basketball for

the Costa Mesa Warriors and playing soccer for Newport Mesa.

   Every Sunday, the 5-foot 6-inch Whitfield _____ her basketball skills
                                       5. displays / is displaying

at various gyms around the county. Head Coach George Grant says Jillianne is a creator on the

court. Creating shots and making crisp passes are reasons her teammates compare her to Michael

Jordan.

   "Jillianne _____ consistently around the ball and she plays good defense," he
           6. is being / is

said. "But her most valued basketball skill is her ability to drive the lane and make off-balance lay-

ups[2] on both sides of the basket, which is why her teammates gave her the name of Ms. Jordan."

   Jillianne laughs at the name, but she likes it.

   "I guess my lay-ups resemble Michael Jordan's," said Jillianne, who right now

_____ 10 points and seven rebounds[3] a game. "Kristin started calling me Ms.
  7. has averaged / is averaging
Jordan and then the rest of them started calling me the name and it stuck."

   Today, basketball _____ Jillianne's time, so she's off to the soccer
                  8. hasn't taken up / isn't taking up
fields, a sport she got into by mistake.

"My younger sister signed up and then didn't want to play, so I took her place," she said. "But on the soccer field, I'm not the star. I'm average."

On the red dirt diamond, Jillianne is one of the stars. The All-Star team _____

9. picks / has picked

Jillianne for the last three years, and she takes pride in her fielding, rather than her offensive game.

"I _____ to play defense. I consider myself a better fielder[4] than a batter,[5]" said

10. like / am liking

Jillianne, who plays first and third base.

Jillianne wants to continue to play baseball in high school in a couple of years.

"I'm going to try out for boys' baseball, but if I don't make it, I'll switch to basketball."

[1] **diamond** baseball playing field

[2] **lay-ups** basketball shots near the basket

[3] **rebounds** catching the basketball after a missed shot

[4] **fielder** baseball player in the field; not at bat

[5] **batter** baseball player at bat

CHAPTER 2 Past Time Tenses

Read the following selection from OC Metro Magazine. *Choose the correct form of the verb.*

Beethoven by the Numbers

Ba-ba-ba-bumm.[1] The four most recognizable notes in music history are those that begin his Fifth Symphony. He was emotional, passionate, charming, and intense—a complicated man of few words but many ideas. He didn't set out to change the world, but as Elvis and the Beatles

_____ the course of popular music in the twentieth century, so Ludwig van

1. changed / were changing

Beethoven altered nineteenth-century music. Throughout his life, he developed musical stepping stones that will forever influence future generations of musicians.

Beethoven _____ born in Bonn, Germany, on December 16, 1770, and was raised

2. had been / was

by an alcoholic father who gave young Beethoven piano lessons so he could become a child prodigy[2] like Mozart and earn money for the family. Beethoven took lessons from Mozart in 1787 and from such musical geniuses as Haydn, Albrechtsberger, and Salieri. He _____ permanently

3. was moving / moved

to Vienna in 1792 and began to compose in earnest. His last work was completed at Gneisendorf in

1826, where he _____ a severe chill and died in March of 1827.

4. developed / was developing

He _____ a friend about his growing deafness in 1801, and by 1818 he was
5. written / wrote

totally deaf. Amazingly, from 1818 to his death he _____ to compose some
6. continued / had continued

of his best works.

In addition to his deafness, Beethoven was considered physically unattractive and

arrogant. In his 1910 work, "A History of Music," musicologist and author Paul Landormy

provides an interesting description of Beethoven: "He was small . . . with . . . grayish-blue eyes so

deep that they _____ black. His smile _____ kind, his laugh
7. were seeming / seemed   8. was being / was

menacing,[3] his nature melancholy.[4]"

In spite of, or perhaps because of, his suffering and tortured nature, Beethoven

_____ highly emotional music that was both revolutionary and respectful of traditional
9. creates / created

classical style. He _____ in love easily, yet his love affairs were unhappy ones, and the
10. fell / falled

joy and sorrow of these loves were reflected in his music.

"His music speaks to humanity," says Dean Corey, Philharmonic Society Executive

Director. "Beethoven is as strong as ever. He's spanned two centuries, and how many things have

done that? He had wanted to move people with his music. I heard someone say that men possess

talent, but genius possesses the man, and Beethoven's music certainly reflects that."

[1]*Ba-ba-ba-bum* the sound of the first few notes of Beethoven's Fifth Symphony

[2]**child prodigy** a child who is extremely good at doing something

[3]**menacing** threatening, troublesome

[4]**melancholy** sad

CHAPTER 3 Subject-Verb Agreement

Read the following selection from Coast *magazine. Choose the the correct form of the verb.*

A Very Able Crew

The rolling decks of a sailboat may seem the most unfriendly of environments for a wheelchair,

but don't tell that to Captain Duncan Milne. For twenty years—since he rode a motorcycle

off a cliff in a desert race and lost the use of his legs—he _____ proven critics
1. has / have

wrong from the decks of his 62-foot traditional ketch.[1] Since 1990 he has put that spirit

to good use, running Access To Sailing, a program that _____ over
2. introduce / introduces

500 children and adults with disabilities to sailing each year. So who better to inspire a crew of five developmentally disabled overachievers to compete in this year's Newport to Ensenada Race? That's right, for the second year running, Milne will lead Team Independence in the 400-boat yacht regatta.[2]

Though Milne's shipmates are challenged with autism, Down syndrome, and slight mental retardation,[3] don't think they will make any excuses if they _____ finish well.
3. don't / doesn't
"We're competing to win, no doubt about it," says Milne. Which is why he and his crew

_____ trained for the race for months, and recently circumnavigated[4] Catalina Island
4. have / has
from Dana Point, traveling 102 miles, much of it in bad weather conditions. "I was really proud of the crew," says Milne.

Tracy Young, manager of community relations for Project Independence, which aids those with developmental disabilities, _____ the crew members couldn't be more thrilled.
5. say / says
"They know that yachting is a pretty exclusive sport, so to be a part of the preparation and race is a chance of a lifetime." And they earned it. Two of the crew sailed in last year's race, and all had to try out for this year's team by undergoing physical fitness and memory tests. Out of over 30 applicants, five made the team.

Though their training _____ mostly been on Milne's ketch, Team Independence
6. has / have
will sail a $1.5 million 43-foot trimaran.[5] Training for the race _____ as much as
7. costs / cost
$10,000 says Young; donations _____ it possible.
8. makes / make
Milne says they _____ backing a winner, regardless of the results. "Sometimes
9. is / are
it can get a little frustrating out there," he says. "But then I consider what an incredible effort they have all made and how far they have come. Suddenly little errors in steering _____
10. isn't / aren't
a big deal—so we come in third instead of first."

[1] **ketch** a type of sailing boat with two masts for the sails

[2] **yacht regatta** a sailboat race

[3] **retardation** slow mental development

[4] **circumnavigated** gone completely around

[5] **trimaran** a boat with three hulls/floats

CHAPTER 4 Expressing Future Time

Read the following selection from New University, *the student newspaper from the University of California, Irvine. Choose the correct form of the verb.*

Arts in the "Real World"

Most students look forward to their post-college lives with a mixture of excitement and trepidation.[1]

For majors in the arts, going out into the "real world" means competing with other dancers, actors, musicians, and artists with years more experience. The excitement of doing what you love for a living is tempered[2] with the realization that the artist's life is often very difficult.

The *New University* interviewed several graduating seniors from the School of the Arts on their hopes and worries for the future, and their experiences at the university.

New University: What are your plans after graduation?

Sarah Reece (Dance): After I graduate, I _____ certified in Pilates.[3] I'm

1. get / will get

going to train other people and support myself while I _____ in New York.

2. audition / will audition

I _____ to New York to audition for modern companies and teach as soon as my

3. am moving / move

certification is completed.

Andrew Henkes (Drama): I _____ begin by applying for positions

4. am going / am going to

as assistant directors or really any positions in theater companies. I'm going to try to find a theater

company or two or three that I like and I _____ them and let them know

5. contact / am going to contact

that I'm interested in working.

Even if I get stuck[4] waiting tables or something, I _____ some theater

6. am going to do / do

work on my own.

Lara Wallis (Music): I'm going to pursue graduate studies at the Manhattan School of

Music in New York City. I _____ oboe with the principal oboist of the New

7. am going to study / study

York Philharmonic when I get to New York.

New University: How well do you think your arts education has prepared you to go out

into the real world?

Henkes: I feel like I've learned a lot. It's hard to say, though. I really

_____ until I get out there.

8. am not knowing / won't know

Wallis: I think it's prepared me in terms of independence, like establishing a home away from the place I originally grew up. I think it has prepared me to go to the East Coast and live away from friends and family. The program in Manhattan _____ many

9. will provide / will provides

challenges, but I feel like I have been ready to make that step forward.

New University: Do you have any worries or concerns about your plans?

Reece: Like any job, there is a lot of competition and I think it _____ be a

10. will / going to

struggle, but I'm looking forward to it.

[1]trepidation fear, dread

[2]tempered softened or moderated

[3]Pilates a specific exercise program

[4]get stuck unable to get away from a boring or unpleasant situation

CHAPTER 5 Time Shifts and Tense

Read the following selection from The Daily Californian, *the school newspaper of the University of California, Berkeley. Choose the correct form of the verb.*

The Ups and Downs of Becoming a Professor

If you are not already burned out on academia[1] by the end of final exams, perhaps you are ready to head toward a future as a professor.

"If you care about ideas, academia is the best place in the world to be," says Michael Nacht, professor and dean of UC Berkeley's School of Public Policy. "As a professor you _____ to

1. get / got

work on whatever you want to work on, in an amazing environment."

Many professors _____ new responsibilities and rise within the ranks[2] of

2. take on / took on

academia by accepting the position of department chair.

As part of his service to the campus, Steven Weber, a political science professor, says he accepted a position as chair of the Center for Western European studies.

In the case of Robert Berdahl, he _____ his career by becoming a history

3. started / starts

professor at the University of Oregon before eventually taking on the responsibility of being UC Berkeley's chancellor.

Some academics[3] choose the teaching profession as a powerful means of entry into the political arena. Haas School of Business Dean Laura d'Andrea Tyson, a former UC Berkeley economics professor, _____ the National Economic Adviser in 1993—the
4. became / becomes
highest-ranking woman in the Clinton administration at the time.

Overall, the job market for becoming a professor _____ more
5. had become / has become
uncertain since the 1970s, when there _____ a boom in government-funded academic
6. is / was
research. As George Will _____ recently, there is a "glut[4] of Ph.Ds,[5]" with
7. has written / had written
larger numbers of people applying for a smaller number of jobs.

According to Nacht, job security and gaining tenure[6] within the profession are difficult. Professors may still find themselves without tenure at age 40 and may have to hustle to be engaged[7] by another university.

"Get published," says Andrew Green, a Ph.D counselor at the Cal Career Center. "There are situations where twenty years ago getting published _____ that
8. is not / was not
important, but because of the recent competition, expectations _____
9. have increased / had increased
dramatically."

Although a strained family life _____ something many working professionals
10. was / is
must deal with, professors say that family life can actually be easier than in other professions because the time schedule _____ more flexible.
11. was / is
"It's fairly easy to take time off from teaching and pick up again later," computer science professor Katherine Yelick says. She adds that she _____ 80-hour weeks until she
12. works / used to work
and her husband, a professor, _____ two young children.
13. had / have

[1]**academia** life or environment at university or college

[2]**rise within the ranks** get promoted in

[3]**academics** college or university teachers

[4]**glut** oversupply, too many

[5]**Ph.D** someone with a Doctor of Philosophy degree, the highest university degree that can be earned

[6]**tenure** a permanent position

[7]**hustle to be engaged** work hard to get hired

CHAPTER 6 Count and Noncount Nouns

Read the following selection from the Daily Bruin, *the newspaper of the University of California, Los Angeles. Choose the correct noun form.*

Point, Click, Buy

Nearly $6 billion will be spent this year—not in stores, boutiques, or shops—but through computer terminals all over the world.

According to many _____, the amount of money spent on on-line
1. researcher / researchers
shopping doubles every year, making it the newest shopping craze.

"On line, you can buy anything," said Emily Wu, a second- _____ sociology
2. year / years
student.

Spending a few minutes on line, shoppers can buy books, clothes, CDs, videos, video games, computer programs, cars, houses, _____ tickets, and nearly anything with a price tag.
3. plane / planes

One major _____ people give for shopping over the Internet is convenience.
4. reason / reasons
The _____ of sitting at home at any hour and selecting products on a screen appeals
5. ease / eases
to many.

"It can be very convenient; you just click on something you like on the screen and it comes to your house in a few days or weeks," Wu said.

Like the Internet itself, though, on-line shopping has its critics.

Although some shopping sites offer sales and discounts on _____
6. merchandise / merchandises
bought online, high shipping and handling[1] charges discourage some on-line shoppers.

"I bought three _____ and spent $30 dollars on shipping and handling," said
7. jacket / jackets
Jessica May, a first-year design student.

Shipping and handling _____ range from usually around $3 for CDs and books
8. charges / charge
to more than 15 percent of the total price on larger purchases.

Another reason Internet _____ spend online is the selection available.
9. shopper / shoppers
"It's such a sense of accomplishment to find something good to buy online, there is just so much to choose from," said Eduardo Puelma, a first-year undeclared student.

Variety of selection is another reason for the high volume of Internet sales. Certain CD and book sites claim millions of _____ to choose from.
10. title / titles

In addition to offering a large _____, clothing sites often offer items not

11. selection / selections

available in stores. This becomes a problem, however, when consumers try to return the item to

the store that runs the web site. Some stores will not take back items bought on line.

With on-line sales increasing every year, it appears as though more _____ will

12. person / people

be turning to the computer screen for their purchases, leaving the malls to frozen yogurt lovers.

[1]**shipping and handling** money you must pay to have something sent to your home

CHAPTER 7 Articles and Other Determiners

Read the following selection from the Daily Pilot *newspaper. Choose the correct article, quantifier, demonstrative adjective, or possessive adjective.*

A Good Impression

Standing in front of Vincent van Gogh's famous painting "The Potato Eaters," Janella Godoy

considered _____ painting thoughtfully before making a pronouncement: "The

1. the / a / Ø

painting is so dark. It is meant to convey sadness. And look at the brush strokes."

Not bad for a sixth-grader at the Los Angeles County Museum of Art for _____

2. the / a / Ø

first time. And scattered throughout the museum's galleries where the sold-out "Van Gogh's Van

Goghs" show is temporarily visiting from the Van Gogh Museum in Amsterdam were

_____ pint-sized[1] art critics.

3. many / much

They're _____ feet shorter and several hundred dollars less-expensively

4. a little / a few

appointed[2] than most of the other museum-goers. And they haven't mastered the fine art of

pretentiously propounding[3] over paintings—one young man referred to "that beautiful painting,

The 'Potato Heads,' or whatever."

But the 85 students from Harbor View Elementary School who spent Friday at

_____ museum have an appreciation of why Van Gogh was _____ great artist.

5. the / a / Ø **6. the / a / Ø**

"His work is very interesting because of the way he uses colors and his brush strokes,"

said Camilla Mooshayedi. "And he experimented with _____ art. First he was

7. the / an / Ø

_____ impressionist[4] painter, and then he picked up other things."

8. the / an / Ø

The sixth-graders at Harbor View are such art fans that they raised the money for buses

and tickets to the museum by selling another one of their favorite things: candy.

"I'm amazed and so proud of them," said teacher Sharon Harrington, who along with teacher Scottia Evans organized _____ trip. "You never know how much they're

9. the / a / Ø

listening, because they're sixth-graders and they have to be so cool. But they really know a lot."

To prepare themselves to understand the paintings, _____ students in

10. the / a / Ø

_____ sixth grade classes tried their hand at Van Gogh's style.

11. this / these

"_____ student painted 'Starry Night,'" one sixth-grader said.

12. Several / Every / Many

A docent[5] came over to _____ students.

13. the / a / Ø

"Sorry. 'Starry Night' is in Minneapolis," he said.

No matter, shrugged the students. They had their own copies at home, and four rooms of one Van Gogh after another to appreciate stretching out before them.

[1]**pint-sized** small, young

[2]**appointed** dressed

[3]**pretentiously propounding** discussing in an exaggerated and showy way

[4]**impressionist** a style of painting that creates effects with color

[5]**docent** a person who leads tours through museums or galleries

CHAPTER 8 Pronouns

Read the following selection from Orange County Woman *magazine. Choose the correct pronoun or possessive adjective.*

Giving Back the Gift

When Santa Ana policemen cleaned out a crime-infested neighborhood five years ago,

_____ knew their job wasn't quite done. Scared residents . . . needed reassurance[1] that

1. they / it

the area was safe again.

So the police department asked Virginia Avila, a mother of seven who lived in the Flower

Street Park neighborhood, to help _____ reclaim[2] the formerly drug-ridden park. With

2. it / them

Avila at the helm[3] of a new neighborhood association, the park has been transformed.

Like Avila, the women whose stories appear here have different histories and life paths.

But they share a deep sense of giving back to the community that nurtured _____

3. themselves / them

with gifts of time, money, and personal example. With those gifts in mind, these women look

forward to focusing on Latino youth.

Sofia Negron: The work that Sofia Negron does as community outreach director for MOMS (Maternal Outreach Management System) Resource Center is worlds away[4] from her previous profession: assistant designer at Ocean Pacific sportswear.

Now _____ can be found recruiting both care providers and clients for
<u>4. she / it</u>
MOMS, a Santa Ana based non-profit organization that offers medical care, education, and support countywide to indigent[5] women who are pregnant or have just had their babies.

" _____ totally changed my life," she says of her career change six years ago.
<u>5. They / It</u>

Sandy Garcia: The title of Sandy Garcia's first CD translates as *Stop Thinking*. But
_____ isn't advice she's taking. When Garcia, 18, isn't singing at mariachi gigs or recording
<u>6. that / those</u>
her new CD in Tijuana, _____ often can be found performing free for charity fund raisers
<u>7. her / she</u>
or serving as a student representative on the county's Human Relations Commission.

Teresa Saldivar: Teresa Saldivar sells jewelry, but that hardly tells her whole story. She's a mainstay[6] in the Hispanic business community, co-chair for the Orange County Hispanic Education Endowment Fund and a role model for both Latino and female business owners. Hispanic leaders she met in college reinforced her faith in education. " _____ inspired me to continue, and
<u>8. They / He</u>
when I opened my own business, I wanted to do the same thing for Hispanic youth. There's a need for _____ to have a role model."
<u>9. them / it</u>

Maria Elena Avila: Maria Elena Avila is in the restaurant business—one of the toughest, most time-consuming professions around. _____ family's seven-restaurant El Ranchito
<u>10. Her / Hers</u>
chain is a Southern California institution,[7] and Avila owns both the Costa Mesa location and El Ranchito's high-end catering business.

Avila, 45, also is a founding member of the Orange County Hispanic Education Endowment Fund, which recently passed its $1 million goal.

[1] **reassurance restored confidence**

[2] **reclaim to make something usable again**

[3] **at the helm in control**

[4] **worlds away very different or far from**

[5] **indigent very poor**

[6] **mainstay main support or help**

[7] **Southern California institution well known in Southern California**

CHAPTER 9 Modals

Read the following selection from the Daily Bruin, *the school newspaper from the University of California, Los Angeles. Choose the correct modal and verb combination.*

This Time, the Interviewer Is in the Spotlight

It is intelligent and warm, understanding and sympathetic. Terry Gross' voice has been heard with some of the most famous people of our time, ranging from Wilt Chamberlain and Hillary Rodham Clinton to Tom Stoppard and Eric Clapton.

This Sunday, the host of National Public Radio's "Fresh Air" will be in Royce Hall to share clips from a few interviews that went particularly well, but mostly from those that should have gone well but were real catastrophes.[1] Though known for her sincerity toward her guests, she is not afraid to ask tough questions and has had her share of walkouts.

It _____ be hard to imagine someone walking out on an interviewer with
1. had better / may
such a friendly and calming voice, but Gross does not see it that way. Actually, the first time she heard her voice on the radio was during a recorded show. Aside from her roommates, Gross didn't tell anyone the program was airing. She felt the experience would be easier to survive if nobody listened.

"My brother called in the middle of the first program, and I told him that I was in the middle of a very important conversation and I just _____ talk," Gross says.
2. can't / couldn't
"I _____ lie to him. I _____ tell him that the program was on."
3. had to / must   **4. couldn't / shouldn't**
Gross says she used to listen to her programs during her 30-minute commute home from work. However, she now lives only five minutes away. Gross

_____ to tapes of shows for a "best of" or
5. may still occasionally listens / may still occasionally listen
anthology[2] program.

"But there are times when the last thing in the world I want to do is hear an interview again," Gross says. "Sometimes I think the unhealthiest thing I _____ do is to spend an
6. ought to / can
hour listening to myself on air."

By now however, Gross has accepted her voice. She says that though it does not mean she loves it, now she _____ listen to it. After all, Gross began hosting "Fresh Air" in 1985,
7. can / can't
when it was a weekly half-hour program.

In 1987, though, the show turned into a daily, hour-long program. This means that Gross

now _____ conduct two interviews a day, prepare for upcoming interviews, and perform
    8. must / have to

other duties for the program, for which she is also a co-executive producer.

    Gross says she reads as much as she can about a guest to prepare for an interview. She

_____ the artists' various movies or listen to their records several times.
9. must also rent / must also rented

Gross does as much as she _____ but says that she still doesn't have as much preparation
    10. could / can

time as she would like.

    [1]**catastrophes** dramatic events or disasters

    [2]**anthology** a collection of literary pieces or programs

CHAPTER 10 Verb Forms, Gerunds, and Infinitives

Read the following selection from Orange County Woman *magazine. Choose the correct verb form, gerund, or infinitive.*

Touched by an Angel

Growing up poor in a Hispanic barrio,[1] Marie Moreno attended a segregated,[2] all-Latino elementary

school. But it wasn't until she moved into an integrated school that she felt true discrimination.

    Moreno, the third youngest of six children, was pelted with beer cans and racist remarks

when she walked to her new school in the third grade in the late 1940s. During classes she was

reprimanded for _____ Spanish. Even when her family eventually moved into a
    1. speaking / to speak

better, predominantly white neighborhood, many children were prohibited from _____
                                           2. play / playing

with her.

    It was at this new school, which was forced _____ as a result of federal
                                       3. integrating / to integrate

legislation, that Moreno recognized a consequence of discrimination: The education she was denied.

    "When I walked into these classes in the new, integrated school, I didn't _____
                                               4. knew / know

what they were talking about. I realized I was so far behind. It made me _____ we had
                                       5. realize / realized

not been getting the education we were supposed to be getting," says Moreno, now 55.

    At age eight she told her parents she wanted _____ the best private
                                    6. attend / to attend

parochial school.[3] When her parents told her they could not _____ the college prep
                                       7. afford / afforded

school, the young Moreno informed them she already had a job—at the local Catholic church.

With the help of her local priest, Moreno worked as the assistant housekeeper on weekends, and over several years saved what at the time was a grand sum: about $800. The nuns and priests helped her _____ for the entrance exam since she had no parochial
8. prepare / preparing
education. After she was accepted in 1959, the nuns helped her sew her own school uniforms while she worked nights and weekends.

After graduation Moreno attended college. Over the next decade she held a series of jobs, where she built her marketing and public relations skills. Through a friend, Moreno learned of an opening with the Anaheim Angels[4] in 1993, and was hired from among seven-hundred applicants, mainly because of her involvement with the Hispanic community. Moreno has

_____ integral in numerous outreach programs, including the "Rookie Ball" program
9. being / been
that allows low-income children _____ on baseball teams for free, as well as
10. to play / playing
other Angels-sponsored free baseball clinics.

Moreno spends much of her time talking to students in the schools and encourages them

_____ their educations. "When I talk to kids, I always let them _____
11. to pursue / pursuing   **12. know / to know**
my background, where I was born and raised and that when they have a dream, the only one that can stop that dream is themselves," she says.

[1] **barrio** area in a city where many poor people live

[2] **segregated** separated from different groups or races

[3] **private parochial school** church school not part of free public school system

[4] **Anaheim Angels** professional baseball team in California

CHAPTER 11 Word Forms

Read the following selection from the Daily Pilot *newspaper. Choose the correct forms. If necessary, use a dictionary to check the correct word form for the part of speech.*

Amputation[1] Leads to Awakening for Pitcher

It's a dream most boys relish at one point in their childhood—playing for a professional baseball team. Like those boys, Dave Dravecky also yearned to make it to the big leagues.

He tasted _____ at various times during his eight-year major league career.
1. success / successful
He was an All-Star and pitched in the playoffs and World Series. Every year life was _____
2. good / better
than the one before for the native of Youngstown, Ohio.

But when a growth was found on the upper part of his arm, Dravecky's priorities suddenly changed. The one tool that got him to the big leagues was _____ taken from him

3. painful / painfully

when the south-paw[2] had his left arm amputated 10 years ago.

"The initial thought was, 'Why me?'" he said. "When the doctors discovered the lump in my arm, they told me I was never going to pitch again outside of a _____. But I did."

4. miraculous / miracle

If _____ a sports fan, the name Dave Dravecky is vaguely familiar. His name

5. you're / your

is synonymous with _____ and courage. Dravecky, 43, was one of the

6. determined / determination

_____ players with the San Diego Padres and then the San Francisco Giants

7. popularest / most popular

when a trainer spotted the lump on his arm. It wasn't until two years later, when he had an arm tendon injury, that a magnetic-resonance-imaging test revealed a _____ tumor

8. cancer / cancerous

in his prized left arm. The tumor would be removed, doctors said, but Dravecky wouldn't play baseball again.

After 50% of his deltoid muscle was removed, he began strengthening his arm. He returned to an overflowing crowd in Candlestick Park. His comeback looked promising. Five days later, the world saw an image that is still in the minds of baseball fans. Dravecky was in the middle of his delivery[3] against the Montreal Expos in Olympic Stadium when his arm snapped in half. The tumor was back, and this time doctors feared it would spread. They decided to _____ his arm.

9. amputate / amputation

"My life was a fairy tale that blew up in my face," he said. "I was face to face with cancer. One thing you learn about cancer is how little control you have over _____ life."

10. your / you're

Dravecky began writing books and speaking to groups. He and wife, Jan, pledged to assist people in a time of need. Their group's volunteer staff has counseled and helped more _____ 2,000 cancer victims. He said offering encouragement to them is

11. then / than

_____ to recovery.

12. essential / essentially

[1]**amputation** removal of an arm or leg

[2]**south-paw** left-handed baseball pitcher

[3]**delivery** baseball pitch

APPENDIX 2 Irregular Verbs

Base Form	Simple Past	Past Participle	Base Form	Simple Past	Past Participle
be	was, were	been	hang	hung	hung
beat	beat	beaten/beat	have	had	had
become	became	become	hear	heard	heard
begin	began	begun	hide	hid	hidden
bend	bent	bent	hit	hit	hit
bet	bet	bet	hold	held	held
bind	bound	bound	hurt	hurt	hurt
bite	bit	bitten	keep	kept	kept
bleed	bled	bled	know	knew	known
blow	blew	blown	lay	laid	laid
break	broke	broken	lead	led	led
bring	brought	brought	leave	left	left
build	built	built	lend	lent	lent
buy	bought	bought	let	let	let
catch	caught	caught	lie	lay	lain
choose	chose	chosen	light	lit/lighted	lit/lighted
cling	clung	clung	lose	lost	lost
come	came	come	make	made	made
cost	cost	cost	mean	meant	meant
creep	crept	crept	meet	met	met
cut	cut	cut	mistake	mistook	mistaken
deal	dealt	dealt	pay	paid	paid
dig	dug	dug	put	put	put
do	did	done	quit	quit	quit
draw	drew	drawn	read	read	read
eat	ate	eaten	rid	rid	rid
fall	fell	fallen	ride	rode	ridden
feed	fed	fed	ring	rang	rung
feel	felt	felt	rise	rose	risen
fight	fought	fought	run	ran	run
find	found	found	say	said	said
fit	fit	fit	see	saw	seen
flee	fled	fled	seek	sought	sought
fly	flew	flown	sell	sold	sold
forbid	forbade	forbidden	send	sent	sent
forecast	forecast	forecast	set	set	set
forget	forgot	forgotten	shake	shook	shaken
forgive	forgave	forgiven	shed	shed	shed
freeze	froze	frozen	shine	shone/shined	shone/shined
get	got	gotten	shoot	shot	shot
give	gave	given	show	showed	shown
go	went	gone	shrink	shrank/shrunk	shrunk/shrunken
grind	ground	ground	shut	shut	shut
grow	grew	grown	sing	sang	sung

Base Form	Simple Past	Past Participle	Base Form	Simple Past	Past Participle
sit	sat	sat	sweep	swept	swept
sleep	slept	slept	swim	swam	swum
slide	slid	slid	swing	swung	swung
speak	spoke	spoken	take	took	taken
speed	sped/speeded	sped/speeded	teach	taught	taught
spend	spent	spent	tear	tore	torn
spin	spun	spun	tell	told	told
spit	spit/spat	spat	think	thought	thought
split	split	split	throw	threw	thrown
spread	spread	spread	understand	understood	understood
spring	sprang	sprung	undertake	undertook	undertaken
stand	stood	stood	upset	upset	upset
steal	stole	stolen	wake	woke	woken/waked
stick	stuck	stuck	wear	wore	worn
sting	stung	stung	weave	wove	woven
stink	stank/stunk	stunk	weep	wept	wept
strike	struck	struck/stricken	win	won	won
string	strung	strung	wind	wound	wound
strive	strove/strived	striven	withdraw	withdrew	withdrawn
swear	swore	sworn	write	wrote	written

APPENDIX 3 Spelling and Punctuation Rules

It is important to correct spelling errors. This appendix gives you spelling rules, which can assist you in becoming a good speller. It also gives you rules for using apostrophes and for capitalization—two areas related to spelling. Keep this list handy so that you can refer to it while writing.

SPELLING RULES FOR WORDS WITH *IE*

This rhyme gives the rule for using *i* and *e*

Use *i* before *e*
Except after *c*
Or when sounding like *a*
As in n*ei*ghbor and w*ei*gh.

Words with *ie*

bel*ie*ve	ch*ie*f
f*ie*ld	gr*ie*f

Words with *ei* after *c*

rec*ei*ve	rec*ei*pt
c*ei*ling	dec*ei*t

Words with *ei* sounding like *a*

fr*ei*ght	v*ei*n
r*ei*gn	n*ei*ghbor

Exceptions

*ei*ther	n*ei*ther
l*ei*sure	s*ei*ze
w*ei*rd	h*ei*ght
for*ei*gn	forf*ei*t

SPELLING RULES FOR SUFFIXES

- When adding *-ing* or another suffix that begins with a vowel or *-y*, drop the final silent *-e.*

achieve + -ing	→	achiev*ing*
locate + -ion	→	locat*ion*
ice + -y	→	ic*y*

Exceptions

change*able*	notice*able*
mile*age*	ey*eing*

- When adding *-ing,* change *-ie* to *-y.*

die	→	d*ying*
tie	→	t*ying*
lie	→	l*ying*

- When adding a suffix that begins with a consonant, keep the final silent *-e.*

discourage + -ment	→	discourage*ment*
sincere + -ly	→	sincere*ly*

Exceptions

argu*ment*	nin*th*
tru*ly*	whol*ly*

- When a word ends in a consonant + *-y,* change *-y* to *-i* before adding a suffix.

funny + -er/-est	→	funn*ier,* funn*iest*
try + -ed	→	tr*ied*
allergy + -ic	→	allerg*ic*

Do not make this change if the suffix is *-ing.*

carry	→	carry*ing*

- When a word ends in a vowel + *-y,* keep the *-y.*

delay	→	delay*ed*

- When a word has one syllable and ends in a single vowel + consonant, double the final consonant.

pen	→	pen*ned*
big	→	big*ger,* big*gest*
sit	→	sit*ting*

- When a word has more than one syllable and ends in a single vowel + consonant, do not double the final consonant.

happen	→	happen*ed*
focus	→	focus*ing*
commit	→	commit*ment*

SPELLING RULES FOR PLURALS

- When making most nouns plural, add -s.

    girl   →   girls
    radio   →   radios

- When a noun ends in -ch, -sh, -s, or -x, add -es.

    church   →   churches
    fox   →   foxes

- When a noun ends in a consonant + -o, add -es.

    potato   →   potatoes
    hero   →   heroes

- When a noun ends in a consonant + -y, drop the -y and add -ies.

    lady   →   ladies
    tragedy →   tragedies

SPELLING RULES FOR PREFIXES

Add a prefix to the beginning of a word without doubling or dropping letters.

    satisfy →   dissatisfy
    behave   →   misbehave
    natural →   unnatural

CAPITALIZATION RULES

Rules for capitalization include the following:

1. Capitalize the first word of each sentence.

2. Capitalize proper nouns (nouns that name specific people, places, groups, and things, including languages, and religious, ethnic, and political groups).

    Adeline Yen Mah, Vancouver, Spanish, Moslems, Hispanic, Democrats

3. Capitalize adjectives of nationality and regional or religious affiliation.

    Brazilian restaurant, Basque region, Christian church

4. Capitalize titles before proper names.

    Professor William Su, Reverend Hoffman, Uncle Joe

5. Capitalize important words in titles of books, plays, movies, newspapers, magazines, songs, etc.

    Romeo and Juliet, The Sound of Music, The Daily Mirror, Newsweek

6. Capitalize historical events and periods.

    Korean War, the Cold War, Renaissance

7. Capitalize holidays, days, and months.

    Easter, Monday, January

8. Do not capitalize seasons.

    summer, spring, winter, fall/autumn

APOSTROPHE RULES

1. Use an apostrophe to show one or more letters have been left out.

    cannot   →   can't
    that is →   that's
    we are   →   we're

2. Use an apostrophe to show ownership.

    the book of the student   → the student's book

    the home of James   → James's home

    the offices of the professors → the professors' offices

APPENDIX 4 Prepositions

A preposition connects a noun or a pronoun to the rest of a sentence. It indicates a relationship such as time, place, or position.

TYPES OF PREPOSITIONS

Here are some common prepositions, listed by the type of relationship they indicate:

1. Prepositions of time

month/year	*in*	Aidan arrived in Yorktown *in* June. He arrived *in* 1999.
day/date	*on*	He began classes *on* Monday. He began class *on* June 5.
specific time	*at*	The classes started *at* 9:00 A.M.
general time	*in*	The classes ended *in* the evening/afternoon/morning.
	before	She left *before* lunch.
	after	I am leaving *after* the exam.
approximate time	*about*	I'll be home *about* 2:00 P.M.
	around	Let's meet *around* 5:00 P.M.
	between	He said he'll call *between* nine and ten o'clock.
duration	*for*	My family lived in Guam *for* six years.
	through	I have thought of you often *through* the years.
	during	We ate a lot of popcorn *during* the movie.

2. Prepositions of place

city/country	*in*	Fred lived *in* Toronto for three years. He lived *in* Canada for five years.
street	*on*	He worked *on* Battery Street.
address	*at*	He lives *at* 16 Queen Lane.
motion	*to*	He goes *to* the park for lunch. (*walk to, run to, drive to, ride to, race to, fly to*)
motion in a direction	*toward*	They walked *toward* me.

3. Prepositions of position

The book is *on* the desk.

The lecture notes are *in* my notebook.

Let's meet *at* the library.

The dog is sitting *beside* its owner.

My house is *between* the library and the bridge.

Some other prepositions that commonly show position are: *above, across, against, along, among, behind, below, beneath, beyond, by, down, inside, into, near, outside, over, past, under, up.*

4. Prepositions of manner

She is good *at* speaking foreign languages.

They finished the test *with* ease.

He can understand their accent *by* listening carefully.

5. Prepositions of comparison

We are so close that he is *like* my brother.

The storm made the sky *as* dark *as* night.

6. Preposition of possession

Dino is a good friend *of* mine.

ADJECTIVE + PREPOSITION COMBINATIONS

This list contains some common adjective + preposition combinations. Check an ESL or learner's dictionary under the adjective for any adjective + preposition combinations that are not on this list.

accustomed to	content with	glad about	opposed to	suitable for
afraid of	curious about	good at		superior to
amazed at/by		guilty of	pleased about	surprised
angry at	dependent on		proud of	about/at/by
anxious about	different from	happy about		
ashamed of		homesick for	ready for	terrible at
aware of	eager for		responsible for	tired of
awful at	envious of	inferior to		
	excited about	interested in	sad about	upset with
bad at			safe from	
bored with/by	familiar with	jealous of	satisfied with	worried about
	famous for		sick of	
capable of	fond of	known for	similar to	
concerned about	friendly to		slow at	
	full of	nervous about	sorry for/about	

VERB + PREPOSITION COMBINATIONS

This list contains common verb + preposition combinations. Check an ESL dictionary under the verb for any verb + preposition combinations that you cannot find on this list.

accuse (someone) of
adapt to
admit to
advise against
agree with
apologize for
apply for (something)
apply to (someplace)
approve of
argue about (something)
argue with (someone)
arrive at

believe in
belong to
blame (someone for/
    something on)

care about/for
choose between
combine (something) with
come from
compare (someone/something)
    to/with
complain about (something)
complain to (someone)
concentrate on
consist of
contribute to
cooperate with
count on

deal with
decide on
depend on
die of/from
disapprove of
dream about/of

escape from
excel at
excuse (someone) for

feel like
fight for/about
forget about
forgive (someone) for

glance at
gossip about
graduate from

happen to
hear about/of (something)
hear from (someone)
hide from
hope for

insist on
interfere with
introduce (someone) to
intend to
invite (someone) to

know about

learn from
listen to
live on
look at
look for
look forward to

matter to

object to

participate in
pay for
plan on
prepare for
prevent from
profit from
prohibit (someone) from
protect (someone/something)
    from

read about
recover from
rely on
rescue from
respond to

search for
speak about (something)
speak to/with (someone)
stare at
stop from
subscribe to
substitute for
succeed in

take advantage of
take care of
talk about (something)
talk to/with (someone)
thank (someone) for
think about/of

vote for

wait for
worry about

Your teacher may use symbols to indicate specific error types in your writing. The charts below include symbols, explanations, and sample sentences for some of these errors. You can also use these symbols to help make the necessary corrections while you are editing your own work. The first chart refers to grammar items that are presented in *Eye on Editing 1*. For further explanation and practice, refer to the indicated chapters in *Eye on Editing 1*. The second chart presents other common correction symbols.

CHART 1

Symbol	Meaning	Sample Sentence	Eye on Editing 1
det	determiner error	*det* It is <u>a</u> most interesting book I have read.	Chapter 7
num	noun error (number)	*num* We have enough <u>homeworks</u> to last a week.	Chapter 6
prn	pronoun error	*prn* My friend and <u>me</u> went to the movies.	Chapter 8
ref	unclear pronoun reference	*ref* We enjoyed the book and the movie, but <u>it</u> was more violent.	Chapter 8
s-v	subject-verb agreement error	*s-v* She never <u>go</u> to the library to study.	Chapter 3
t	verb tense error	*t* We <u>haven't completed</u> the project yesterday.	Chapters 1, 2, 4, 5
vb	verb form error	*vb* They <u>haven't went</u> to the gym in weeks.	Chapter 9, 10
wf	word form error	*wf* Her father is the most <u>success</u> software engineer in the firm.	Chapter 11

CHART 2

Symbol	Meaning	Sample Sentence
cs	comma splice; using a comma to connect two sentences	*cs* It was a beautiful day, there wasn't a cloud in the sky.
frag	fragment; a partial sentence punctuated as a complete sentence	*frag* <u>When we practice</u>. The team must work together.
id	problem with idioms or set expressions	*id* We always <u>agree to</u> our teachers.
p	punctuation error	*p* I remember, graduation as the most memorable event.
ro	run on; two or more sentences without punctuation between them	*ro* The lecture was very <u>interesting it</u> went by so fast.
sp	spelling error	*sp* My apartment is <u>noisey</u> and expensive.
ww	wrong word	*ww* He is the best offensive player <u>in</u> the team.
^	insert missing word	They are interested going with us to the concert. ^
ɣ	delete	His writing is clear, and concise, and interesting to read.
¶	paragraph	*¶* This is the prominent theme. A secondary theme explains . . .
//	faulty parallelism	*//* We hoped for relaxation, peace and <u>to have good weather</u>.
#	add a space	*#* My friends went to the club <u>eventhough</u> it's very expensive.
⟲	move here	The book was interesting that I stayed up all night reading.
∿	transpose	We hardly could remember the way to your house.

APPENDIX 6 | Editing Log

Use this editing log or create a similar one of your own to keep track of the grammar errors that you make in your writing. By logging and correcting your errors you will begin to see which errors you make the most. Once you recognize the grammar items that are the most problematic for you, editing becomes easier.

Error	Symbol	Original Sentence	Revised Sentence
Subject-verb agreement	s-v	The essays I wrote about Chinese history was the best in the class.	The essays I wrote about Chinese history were the best in the class.

APPENDIX 7 Grammar Book References

	Eye on Editing 1	*Fundamentals of English Grammar,* Second Edition	*Focus on Grammar, Intermediate,* Second Edition	*Grammar Express,* First Edition
Chapter 1 Present Time Tenses	Chapter 1 Present Time Chapter 7 The Present Perfect and the Past Perfect	Unit 1 Present Progressive and Simple Present Tense Unit 16 Present Perfect: *Since* and *For* Unit 17 Present Perfect: *Already* and *Yet* Unit 18 Present Perfect: Indefinite Past Appendix 2 Common Non-Action (Stative) Verbs	Unit 1 Present Progressive Unit 2 Simple Present Tense Unit 3 Non-Action Verbs Unit 4 Present Progressive and Simple Present Tense Unit 11 Present Perfect: *Since* and *For* Unit 12 Present Perfect *Already* and *Yet* Appendix 2 Common Non-Action (Stative) Verbs
Chapter 2 Past Time Tenses	Chapter 2 Past Time Chapter 7 The Present Perfect and the Past Perfect	Unit 3 Simple Past Tense Unit 4 *Used To* Unit 5 Past Progressive and Simple Past Tense Unit 19 Present Perfect and Simple Past Tense Appendix 1 Irregular Verbs	Unit 6 Simple Past Tense: Affirmative Statements Unit 7 Simple Past Tense: Negative Statements and Questions Unit 8 *Used to* Unit 9 Past Progressive Unit 10 Past Progressive and Simple Past Tense Unit 14 Present Perfect and Simple Past Tense Unit 17 Past Perfect Appendix 1 Irregular Verbs
Chapter 3 Subject- Verb Agreement	Chapter 1 Present Time: 1-2 Chapter 2 Past Time: 2-2, 2-7 Chapter 4 Nouns and Pronouns Chapter 7 The Present Perfect and the Past Perfect: 7-2 Chapter 8 Count / Noncount Nouns; Nouns and Articles	Unit 1 Present Progressive and Simple Present Tense Unit 3 Simple Past Tense Unit 5 Past Progressive and Simple Past Tense Unit 16 Present Perfect: *Since* and *For*	Unit 1 Present Progressive Unit 2 Simple Present Tense Unit 3 Non-Action Verbs Unit 4 Present Progressive Unit 6 Simple Past Tense: Affirmative Statements Unit 7 Simple Past Tense: Negative Statements and Questions Unit 8 *Used to* Unit 9 Past Progressive
Chapter 4 Expressing Future Time	Chapter 3 Future Time	Unit 6 Future Unit 7 Future Time Clauses	Unit 19 Future: *Be going to* and *Will* Unit 20 Future: Contrast Unit 21 Future Time Clauses

Eye on Editing 1	Fundamentals of English Grammar, Second Edition	Focus on Grammar, Intermediate, Second Edition	Grammar Express, First Edition
Chapter 5 Time Shifts and Tense	See References for Chapters 1–4	See References for Chapters 1–4	See References for Chapters 1–4
Chapter 6 Count and Noncount Nouns	Chapter 4 Nouns and Pronouns: 4-1, 4-5 Chapter 8 Count / Noncount Nouns and Articles	Unit 37 Nouns and Quantifiers Unit 38 Articles: Indefinite and Definite	Unit 56 Nouns Unit 57 Quantifiers Unit 58 Articles: Indefinite and Definite Unit 59 Ø (No Article) and *The*
Chapter 7 Articles and Other Determiners	Chapter 4 Nouns and Pronouns Chapter 8 Count / Noncount Nouns and Articles	Units 38 Articles: Indefinite and Definite	Unit 58 Articles: Indefinite and Definite Unit 59 Ø (No Article) and *The*
Chapter 8 Pronouns	Chapter 4 Nouns and Pronouns Chapter 8 Count / Noncount Nouns and Articles	Unit 9 Reflexive and Reciprocal Pronouns Appendix 3 Verbs and Expressions Commonly Used Reflexively	Unit 60 Reflexive Pronouns and Reciprocal Pronouns Appendix 16 Verbs and Expressions Commonly Used Reflexively
Chapter 9 Modals	Chapter 5 Modal Auxiliaries Chapter 11 Passive Sentences: 11-12	Unit 11 Ability: *Can, Could, Be Able To* Unit 12 Permission: *May, Could, Can, Do You Mind If...?* Unit 13 Requests: *Will, Would, Could, Can, Would You Mind...?* Unit 14 Advice: *Should, Ought To, Had Better* Unit 15 Suggestions: *Let's, Could, Why Don't...? Why Not...? How About...?* Unit 32 Preferences: *Prefer, Would Prefer, Would Rather* Unit 33 Necessity: *Have (Got) to, Don't Have to, Must, Must Not, Can't* Unit 34 Expectations: *Be Supposed To* Unit 35 Future Possibility: *May, Might, Could* Unit 36 Assumptions: *Must, Have (Got) To, May, Might, Could, Can't*	Unit 27 Ability: *Can, Could, Be Able To* Unit 28 Permission: *May, Can, Could, Do You Mind If...?* Unit 29 Requests: *Will, Can, Would, Could, Would You Mind...?* Unit 30 Advice: *Should, Ought To, Had Better* Unit 31 Suggestions: *Could, Why Don't...? Why Not...? Let's, How About...?* Unit 32 Preferences: *Prefer, Would Prefer, Would Rather* Unit 33 Necessity: *Have (Got) To and Must* Unit 34 Choice: *Don't have to; No Choice: Must not and Can't* Expectations: *Be Supposed To* Future Possibility: *May, Might, Could* Assumptions: *May, Might, Could, Must, Have (Got) To, Can't*

Eye on Editing 1	Fundamentals of English Grammar, Second Edition	Focus on Grammar, Intermediate, Second Edition	Grammar Express, First Edition
Chapter 10 Verb Forms, Gerunds, and Infinitives	Chapter 1 Present Time: 1-2 Chapter 2 Past Time: 2-2, 2-7 Chapter 4 The Present Perfect and the Past Perfect Chapter 10 Gerunds and Infinitives: 10-1–10-5, 10-7 Chapter 11 Passive Sentences	Unit 26 Gerunds: Subject and Object Unit 27 Gerunds after Prepositions Unit 28 Infinitives after Certain Verbs Unit 29 Infinitives of Purpose Unit 30 Infinitives with *Too* and *Enough* Unit 31 Gerunds and Infinitives Appendix 9 Common Verbs Followed by the Gerund Appendix 10 Common Verbs Followed by the Infinitive Appendix 11 Common Verbs Followed by the Gerund or the Infinitive Appendix 12 Verbs Followed by Objects and the Infinitive	Unit 46 Gerunds: Subject and Object Unit 47 Gerunds after Prepositions Unit 48 Infinitives after Certain Verbs Unit 49 Infinitives after Certain Adjectives and Certain Nouns Unit 50 Infinitives with *Too* and *Enough* Unit 51 Infinitives of Purpose Unit 52 Gerunds and Infinitives Unit 53 *Make, Have, Let, Help* and *Get* Appendix 3 Common Verbs Followed by the Gerund Appendix 4 Common Verbs Followed by the Infinitive Appendix 5 Verbs Followed by the Objects and the Infinitive Appendix 6 Common Verbs Followed by the Gerund or the Infinitive
Chapter 11 Word Forms	Chapter 4 Nouns and Pronouns: 4-5 Chapter 11 Passive Sentences: 11-8–11-9 Chapter 13 Comparisons	Unit 22 Adjectives and Adverbs Unit 23 Adjectives: Comparisons and Equatives Unit 24 Adjectives: Superlatives Unit 25 Adverbs: Equatives, Comparatives, Superlatives Appendix 6 Common Participial Adjectives Appendix 7 Irregular Comparisons of Adjectives, Adverbs, and Quantifiers Appendix 8 Some Adjectives that Form the Comparative and Superlative in Two Ways	Unit 40 Adjectives and Adverbs Unit 41 Participial Adjectives Appendix 10 Irregular Comparisons of Adjectives, Adverbs, and Quantifiers Appendix 11 Common Participial Adjectives Appendix 12 Some Adjectives that Form the Comparative and Superlative in Two Ways

Answer Key

Chapter 1

PRETEST (page 1)

1. love
2. has been
3. remembers
4. ✓
5. is searching

6. ✓
7. work out
8. has studied
9. ✓
10. ✓

SELF CHECK 1 (page 4)

1. doesn't like
2. freezes
3. belongs

4. go
5. has

SELF CHECK 2 (page 6)

1. knows
2. is listening
3. celebrate
4. am taking
5. is driving

SELF CHECK 3 (page 8)

1. haven't slept
2. have driven
3. has been
4. have been sick
5. has . . . gone

EDITING PRACTICE (pages 8–10)

1
1. has become
2. ✓
3. has . . . gone
4. have not lived
5. ✓
6. remembers

7. ✓
8. is studying
9. believe
10. have made
11. is
12. ✓

2
1. is
2. depend
3. brings
4. am going through
5. want

6. am trying
7. play
8. have done
9. know

3
1. is
2. defines
3. has changed
4. has become
5. has undergone

6. live/are living
7. includes
8. has changed
9. have stayed
10. have remained

4
In recent years, academic achievement **has become** the most important sign of success in many cultures. As a result, competition among students and among their parents has increased. This competition **has become/is becoming** difficult for young people to handle. Recently, this **has led** to several societal problems, including suicide. Currently, suicide **is increasing** among students in some countries where academic pressures are high. Many students are failing due to stress, not due to lack of knowledge or effort. However, this intense pressure is producing highly educated and productive members of society in many parts of the world.

Since I arrived in the United States to study, I **have noticed** that academic success is not important to all Americans. Although American society is productive, the emphasis on academic success **is not** as strong as it is in some other countries. This may be because this country has many different cultures, and each culture defines success in a different way. In fact, for many years, when selecting from applicants, American university admissions officers **have considered** a student's school and community involvement in addition to grades. As a result, students are well rounded but may be academically inferior to students in other countries. Because of this problem, American educators **are** now **trying** to increase their academic standards.

All educational systems have positive and negative aspects. We just **need** to take the good parts from systems all over the world and **combine** them to make one truly successful model.

1. loves
2. have played
3. is swinging
4. haven't stopped
5. displays
6. is
7. is averaging
8. isn't taking up
9. has picked
10. like

Chapter 2

PRETEST (page 12)

1. ate
2. hadn't fixed
3. ✓
4. hadn't heard
5. ✓
6. was studying
7. ✓
8. had never flown
9. ✓
10. went

SELF CHECK 1 (page 15)

1. used to watch
2. didn't complete
3. got married
4. When did . . . finish
5. spoke

SELF CHECK 2 (page 16)

1. had
2. was taking
3. was eating
4. was still sleeping
5. joined

SELF CHECK 3 (page 18)

1. had left
2. realized
3. had accepted
4. attended
5. hadn't seen

EDITING PRACTICE (pages 18–20)

1
1. had to move
2. went
3. ✓
4. felt
5. ✓
6. saw
7. ✓
8. got
9. had
10. were living
11. had never taken
12. ✓

2
1. didn't know
2. was taking/took
3. studied
4. graduated
5. overcame
6. was doing
7. found
8. quit
9. was
10. didn't seem

3
1. matured
2. became
3. were flying
4. knew
5. was looking/ looked
6. entered
7. was
8. were adjusting/ adjusted
9. had
10. learned

4 Today I still **remember** the start of my longest friendship. It began in fourth grade. There was a girl in my class named Sandi. She **was** the one who always forgot to raise her hand and who talked loudly to her friends. One day Sandi asked me to help her with her homework. I didn't want to help her, but I didn't know how to say no. I **chose** not to answer her question. I was working quietly when she told the teacher I was her new homework partner. I disliked Sandi, and after a while I **didn't want** to disregard her question. I had ignored her for as long as I could. I walked up to Sandi and told her I was not going to help with her homework. Nobody had ever said no to her before, so she **looked** very surprised. The teacher had heard our conversation, and she came over to talk to me. She said that she needed my help with Sandi, so I **agreed** to be her partner. After I **had worked** with Sandi for a few days, I **learned** that she was very nice, and I **had judged** her too quickly. It's amazing that we are still friends today when I think about how our friendship **started**.

APPENDIX 1: PRACTICE WITH AUTHENTIC LANGUAGE (page 94)

1. changed
2. was
3. moved
4. developed
5. wrote
6. continued
7. seemed
8. was
9. created
10. fell

Chapter 3

PRETEST (page 21)

1. ✓
2. ✓
3. are organizing
4. were
5. Does
6. is
7. ✓
8. ✓
9. offers
10. comes

EDITING PRACTICE (pages 24–25)

1
1. have
2. ✓
3. cost
4. are
5. were
6. ✓
7. require
8. ✓
9. is
10. go
11. is
12. ✓

2
1. have
2. are
3. are
4. put
5. asks for
6. wait
7. become
8. goes/has gone
9. is
10. come

3
1. are
2. is
3. are
4. requires
5. have
6. is
7. is
8. have
9. has
10. is

4 When I first entered high school, I met my best friend for life, Chong. Throughout our four years in high school, we **were** best friends. Now that we are away at different universities, our friendship and affection **have grown** stronger. We **communicate** daily through e-mail. E-mail **helps** us stay in touch over a long distance. Chong is at the University of Chicago, and I am at the University of Southern California, so it is difficult and expensive for us to communicate in any other way. I think my best friend **feels** lonely in Illinois; therefore, I always **take** the time to write him. We have had many experiences together. One of the most memorable events **was** during our senior year. It involved our senior physics final, which neither one of us did well on. There **were** many times we competed against each other, but those times helped us to build a strong friendship. I know Chong **cherishes** our relationship as much as I do. We are both majoring in biology and planning to go to the same medical school. Being apart now **has made** our friendship stronger, and I'm sure our friendship will stay strong in the future.

APPENDIX 1: PRACTICE WITH AUTHENTIC LANGUAGE (page 95)

1. has
2. introduces
3. don't
4. have
5. says
6. has
7. costs
8. make
9. are
10. aren't

Chapter 4

PRETEST (page 27)

1. ✓
2. presents
3. is leaving/leaves/is going to leave
4. is going to garden
5. ✓
6. is going to rain
7. ✓
8. are going to buy/will buy
9. is going to study/will study
10. ✓

EDITING PRACTICE (pages 30–32)

1
1. ✓
2. is going to get/will get
3. will have
4. is going to be/will be
5. are going to arrive
6. ✓
7. will sleep/am going to sleep
8. will remember
9. won't work
10. ✓
11. will rent
12. arrive

2
3. will arrive/are going to arrive
5. are
7. will look/are going to look
9. won't include
11. leave
12. are going to stay
13. will be
16. will contribute/am going to contribute
18. will help
19. graduate

3
1. will take
2. gets
3. are renting
4. will show
5. will see
6. exit
7. will be
8. won't finish
9. will want
10. are going to tour
11. are going to stop
12. will help

4 My friends and I are beginning to think seriously about what we are going to do after we finish our last English class. We definitely know what we are doing right after we take our last exam; it's the distant future that is more uncertain! Immediately after we finish our last exam, a big group of us **will walk** to the nearest arcade to celebrate. The owner has promised us that his arcade will be a good place to start our celebration. We **will spend/are going to spend** an hour or two at the arcade before we go to the next event. Koko and Elena **are having/are going to have** a party and dinner at their apartment. When we get there, we **will go/are going to go** swimming, play darts, horseshoes, and cards, and eat delicious food from all over the world. Each person will bring one dish from his or her country. This way, the food **will taste** exotic. We all know that this **will be/is going to be** a great party and a wonderful way to end our studies together, but there are big questions about our futures that we still need to answer.

After I **say** good-bye to all of my friends at the party, I am going home to pack my bags. I will leave the following day for my next adventure. Even though I **won't know** exactly what I **am going to do** in my uncle's company until I arrive, I plan to use my newly improved English skills. My uncle wants me to work with his English-speaking suppliers and customers since he does not feel comfortable speaking in his second language. My future home will be on another continent. This will be the third I have lived on. I think that I **will love/am going to love** it as much as the first two.

APPENDIX 1: PRACTICE WITH AUTHENTIC LANGUAGE (page 97)

1. will get
2. audition
3. am moving
4. am going to
5. am going to contact
6. am going to do
7. am going to study
8. won't know
9. will provide
10. will

Chapter 5

PRETEST (page 34)

1. ✓
2. begins
3. decided
4. saw
5. will be
6. haven't seen
7. ✓
8. is taking
9. ✓
10. finished/had finished

EDITING PRACTICE (pages 36–38)

1
1. returned
2. ✓
3. received
4. ✓
5. prepared
6. don't
7. ✓
8. have had
9. don't remember
10. ✓
11. ✓
12. bought

2
1. know
2. has
3. surrounds
4. overpowers
5. spent
6. lived
7. took/would take
8. entered/would enter
9. were
10. remember

3
1. was
2. practiced
3. began
4. did not want
5. started
6. is
7. was
8. loved
9. made
10. are
11. hope
12. will remain/remain
13. is
14. has
15. takes up
16. will have
17. went
18. holds

4 Many people are *now* adopting children who are five years old or older from former Soviet countries that can no longer care for their orphans and disabled children. *In the past*, I always **planned** to adopt an infant. I *still* **think** adopting poor and mistreated children is a humanitarian thing to do; however; I am *now* getting a sense of the large sacrifices involved in adopting a child. *A few months ago,* my neighbors adopted a seven-year-old boy from Romania. *Before* I met their new son, I **believed** he was going to be happy to have kind and loving parents. However, *now* I am not so certain. He doesn't know how to respond to love because he never **received** any *in the first few years of his life. By the time he was five,* he **had developed/developed** his own thoughts and behaviors that were appropriate for a child in his situation. In his *current* place in a loving family, these thoughts and behaviors **are** not appropriate. The child is slowly adapting to his new environment, and I am sure in the *next few years* he **will grow** familiar with his new family members and surroundings. I *now* see the unique challenges that adopted children **bring** to families. I *still* believe children are wonderful, and they **increase** the joy in their parents' lives, but *sometimes* adopting children **leads** to unforeseen problems.

APPENDIX 1: PRACTICE WITH AUTHENTIC LANGUAGE (page 98)

1. get
2. take on
3. started
4. became
5. has become
6. was
7. has written
8. was not
9. have increased
10. is
11. is
12. used to work
13. had

Chapter 6

PRETEST (page 40)

1. grammar
2. ✓
3. six-page
4. children
5. times
6. traffic
7. ✓
8. thieves
9. ✓
10. vacation

SELF CHECK 1 (page 42)

1. labs
2. five-paragraph
3. tragedies
4. men
5. matches

SELF CHECK 2 (page 43)

1. vocabulary
2. weather . . . is
3. coffee
4. research
5. information

EDITING PRACTICE (pages 43–45)

1.
1. ✓
2. work
3. ✓
4. Ø bread
5. wives
6. feet
7. ✓
8. were too many
9. ✓
10. ten-foot

2.
1. people
2. stereotypes
3. hair
4. statements
5. sadness
6. generalizations
7. Information
8. education

3.
1. money
2. jewelry
3. advice
4. relatives
5. Excitement
6. travel
7. luggage
8. tickets
9. trips
10. times

4. While I was in high school, I was lucky to have many good **friends**. Unfortunately, some of my friends eventually became more like enemies. During our freshman and sophomore years, there were five of us who shared secrets and never spent a minute apart. We all became friends in our ninth-grade English class because we liked to study **grammar** and read the **five hundred-page** novels that the teacher always assigned. I thought we would be friends forever; however, I was wrong. It started with three **arguments** between two friends who always thought only of themselves and wouldn't share anything—not even **clothing**. These **disagreements** forced our group to split in half by the end of our junior year. I learned many lessons from this experience. One of the things I will always remember is the importance of **honesty**. Friends must tell each other the **truth**. If they tell lies, the friendships that they share will not last. Now I have a new group of five **friends** in college, and I hope these new friendships will last forever. It is impossible for friends to avoid trouble all of the time, but I know the pain of losing **friends** and will do anything to keep my new group together.

APPENDIX 1: PRACTICE WITH AUTHENTIC LANGUAGE (page 100)

1. researchers	7. jackets
2. year	8. charges
3. plane	9. shoppers
4. reason	10. titles
5. ease	11. selection
6. merchandise	12. people

Chapter 7

PRETEST (page 46)

1. the best book	6. ✓
2. ✓	7. ✓
3. the lecture	8. many antiques
4. ✓	9. a bike ride
5. these books	10. a few songs

SELF CHECK 1 (page 49)

1. a good book
2. The exam was hard.
3. the intelligence
4. Ø life
5. the last question

SELF CHECK 2 (page 51)

1. each test
2. much clothing/any clothing
3. any wildflowers/many wildflowers
4. Each sociology test/Each of the sociology tests
5. another day

EDITING PRACTICE (pages 51–53)

1
1. a better grade
2. Ø Thanksgiving
3. ✓
4. every class
5. ✓
6. This test/The test/These tests are
7. any questions
8. Ø ice/some ice
9. another book
10. Each one of the teachers/Each teacher

2
4. an alarm clock
6. Each roommate
7. these differences
10. Ø patience
12. my eyes

3

1. a	8. the
2. a	9. the
3. Ø	10. Ø
4. a	11. the
5. the	12. The
6. the	13. the
7. Ø	14. The

4 We have all been exposed to **many/a lot of** teachers throughout our lives. These teachers come in many forms: schoolteachers, parents, relatives, friends, and neighbors. There are many aspects to being a good teacher. One important job of all teachers is building self-confidence, and **another** job is motivating the students. A lot of students have been motivated by a teacher during their lives. Giving **praise** is one of the most successful ways to help students learn. However, each **teacher** has a unique style for motivating students. Most "A" students are self-motivated or are motivated by good **grades/a** good **grade**. The remaining students need **encouragement/some encouragement** from their teachers. Students spend so much time with them that they need **teachers** to speak kindly and give them guidance. My favorite elementary school teacher was excellent at motivating his students in a positive way, and he achieved very good results from his students with **this** method. Negative motivation may work with a few **students**, but many students work harder and more successfully with some positive reinforcement. Even as a college student, I still need to receive positive feedback from my instructors. I guess it's just human nature to want **encouragement** and praise.

APPENDIX 1: PRACTICE WITH AUTHENTIC LANGUAGE (page 101)

1. the
2. the
3. many
4. a few
5. the
6. a
7. Ø
8. an
9. the
10. the
11. these
12. Every
13. the

Chapter 8

PRETEST (page 55)

1. me
2. I
3. yours
4. their
5. ✓
6. ✓
7. these look
8. ✓
9. them
10. ✓

EDITING PRACTICE (pages 59–61)

1
1. me
2. he or she doesn't want to
3. them
4. ✓
5. it
6. ✓
7. her
8. His parents, who frequently vacation in Hawaii, love tropical weather.
9. ✓
10. I

2
1. their
2. themselves
3. they are
4. . . . the food, which can be hamburgers or hotdogs, is always good.

5. them
6. himself or herself
7. them
8. he or she
9. he or she
10. the others

3
1. I
2. it
3. them
4. it
5. themselves
6. this
7. themselves
8. his
9. they
10. he or she
11. this
12. its
13. their
14. others

4 The Salad Bowl Theory, which describes many societies today, ~~it~~ claims that all immigrants should keep **their** individuality but also add to the dominant culture. This type of society looks like a salad with many different ingredients that all make up one large dish, but each flavor is distinct on its own. Many large cities throughout the world are perfect examples of this theory. These cities have a number of different ethnic communities that live by **themselves**. However, these communities ~~they~~ also contribute to the overall mix of their cities. Every neighborhood has **its** own characteristics, but living together as one large salad helps maintain strong neighborhoods, cities, states, and countries.

Others feel the Melting Pot Theory describes a better way for different cultures to live harmoniously together. This theory states that once an immigrant comes to a new country, **he or she** should leave behind the old culture and traditions. In other words, immigrants must "melt" into the dominant culture. While many immigrant groups in the past have given up **their** culture and language, many groups today fight this theory and try not to lose **theirs**.

Although there are other theories, **these are** two of the most commonly known. It is difficult to say which theory is more common today. The only thing that can be said accurately is that immigrants must be comfortable with **themselves** and with different cultures in order to survive in today's diverse societies.

APPENDIX 1: PRACTICE WITH AUTHENTIC LANGUAGE (page 102)

1. they
2. them
3. them
4. she
5. It
6. that
7. she
8. They
9. them
10. Her

Chapter 9

PRETEST (page 63)

1. should give
2. ✓
3. could play
4. have to study/must study
5. ✓
6. ✓
7. are supposed to
8. were not able
9. ✓
10. can pay

SELF CHECK 1 (page 65)

1. can help
2. have to start
3. should not study
4. has to prepare
5. Does Pat have to go

SELF CHECK 2 (page 67)

1. may not/cannot/must not talk
2. had better not/cannot/must not turn in
3. do not have to take
4. can climb
5. must be closed

EDITING PRACTICE (pages 67–69)

1
1. don't have to do
2. had better pass
3. ✓
4. can call
5. ✓
6. must not ever call
7. could not find
8. ✓
9. had to work
10. ✓

2
2. had to bow
3. must look
4. may seem
5. cannot make
6.
7. had to adapt
8. must learn/have to learn
9. will see

3 Answers may vary. Possible answers include:
1. They might go out for dinner, but it's not certain.

2. The instructor said the students must read the whole textbook this quarter.
3. The writer thinks it's a good idea to learn a second language, but does not have enough time.
4. Tourists are able to eat a lot of good food in Italy.
5. Marcus won't be able to take the SCUBA class unless he learns to swim first.

4 In the novel *Black Boy*, by Richard Wright, the author writes about his own life. Throughout the novel Richard Wright is a very independent person. This **may be** because Richard's father leaves the family when Richard is still a boy. Therefore, Richard **has to be** responsible for doing the household chores and taking care of his younger brother. Richard also **has to stand up** for himself, which is often difficult for a child. Even though he experiences hardship as a child, Richard <u>is able to maintain</u> his curiosity and interest in life. Later, more unhappiness comes to Richard and his family. His mother has a stroke and is partially paralyzed. Richard is forced to take help from the neighbors. Soon after, Richard's grandmother comes to help the family. She **can look after/is able to look after** Richard's mother and brother better than Richard can. Later, other relatives arrive and decide that Grandmother **is not able to watch** Richard's family any longer. After his grandmother leaves, Richard <u>has to live</u> with his Uncle Edward, and Richard's brother goes to live with his Aunt Maggie.

I liked reading this novel about Richard Wright and how he reacts to racial issues in America. The story **may help** readers understand issues that African Americans face in the United States. I prefer learning history through a novel like *Black Boy* to learning through history books. Studying books like *Black Boy* <u>might encourage</u> students to explore complex issues with interest and passion. I **cannot forget** the lessons I learned about racism and hardship from this novel.

APPENDIX 1: PRACTICE WITH AUTHENTIC LANGUAGE (page 104)

1. may
2. couldn't
3. had to
4. couldn't
5. may still occasionally listen
6. can
7. can
8. must
9. must also rent
10. can

Chapter 10

PRETEST (page 70)

1. didn't take
2. haven't bought
3. review
4. ✓
5. avoid driving
6. ✓
7. make me practice
8. ✓
9. ✓
10. miss seeing

SELF CHECK 1 (page 72)

1. Did . . . win
2. aren't
3. is visiting
4. Did you buy
5. can play

SELF CHECK 2 (page 74)

1. dislike eating
2. hopes to see
3. made them feel
4. are excited about joining
5. look forward to swimming

EDITING PRACTICE (pages 74–76)

1
1. ✓
2. let their animals wander
3. ✓
4. helps children behave/to behave
5. doesn't divide
6. ✓
7. is blowing/blows
8. covers
9. been
10. ✓
11. didn't find
12. look forward to finishing

2
1. is living/lives
2. dislike making
3. may make
4. do not like
5. are going to develop/will develop
6. have improved
7. decide to eat
8. let themselves become
9. are preoccupied with losing weight
10. enjoy exercising more
11. helps people eat well/to eat well
12. did not worry

3
1. understand
2. give
3. help
4. adapt/to adapt
5. hope
6. ending
7. move
8. ended
9. to leave
10. thinking/to think
11. trying
12. to prevent

4 Los Angeles is a city that is full of excitement and diversity. It is unfortunate that the city **has received/received** a lot of bad press because of the smog, the crime, and the riots in the early 1990s. Although some negative perceptions of Los Angeles may be accurate, tourists **should not overlook** the city when they make their travel plans. In fact, southern California residents ought to think about **visiting** downtown more often. This area **has become** a center of excitement and diversity. Koreatown, Little Tokyo, and Olvera Street all exist within several square miles of each other. This racial diversity helps Angelenos **understand/to understand** other cultures and beliefs and, in addition, helps them **accept/to accept** differences more easily. The city's art community is also first-rate. Previously, Los Angeles **did not have** a theater district like New York City does, but now there are several theater complexes and many small theaters throughout the city. The one thing Los Angeles **has** always **been** famous for is Hollywood, and it's better than ever. Hollywood is responsible for **entertaining** the world and, like the rest of the city, **promises to impress** visitors and residents alike.

APPENDIX 1: PRACTICE WITH AUTHENTIC LANGUAGE (page 105)

1. speaking
2. playing
3. to integrate
4. know
5. realize
6. to attend
7. afford
8. prepare
9. been
10. to play
11. to pursue
12. know

Chapter 11

PRETEST (page 78)

1. ✓
2. scary
3. quickly
4. ✓
5. passed
6. fastest
7. ✓
8. entire
9. permission
10. ✓

SELF CHECK 1 (page 80)

1. interested
2. carefully
3. successful
4. disappointed
5. reference

SELF CHECK 2 (page 82)

1. most expensive
2. cheaper
3. worst
4. more convenient
5. well

SELF CHECK 3 (page 84)

1. their
2. too
3. affects
4. you're/you are
5. passed

EDITING PRACTICE (pages 84–86)

1
1. diverse
2. embarrassed
3. ✓
4. ✓
5. Responsibility
6. distant
7. ✓
8. happiness
9. richer
10. ✓
11. well
12. most important

2
1. coast
2. except
3. friendly
4. well
5. smarter
6. more foolish
7. exciting
8. most interesting
9. its
10. disappointed
11. than
12. most pleasant

3
1. different
2. cultures
3. traditional
4. dependent
5. financial
6. traditionally
7. gladly
8. graduation
9. best
10. decision
11. significant
12. easier

4 When I am asked to describe myself as a writer, I have a difficult time writing down my thoughts. I am a **slow** writer and find the **toughest** part of an essay to write is the introduction. Sometimes I can sit **impatiently** in front of the computer for hours with only a few words to show for my time. I know writing is a slow process, but I am **frustrated** a lot of the time. Once I am **past** the introduction, I write the body and conclusion more **rapidly**. In fact, to be honest, I almost enjoy writing by the time I finish a paper. It's a big accomplishment, and I always feel proud of myself. In-class writing can be an even bigger problem than out-of-class writing. An essay exam is always **frightening**, especially when I'm given only a short period of time to complete it. I usually write very **slowly** on these tests and never have time to finish. Even though writing makes me feel uncomfortable, I know I have to work on this **important** skill. I definitely plan on becoming a good writer as quickly as possible. My teachers keep telling me that if I write **more often**, I'll be more comfortable and less anxious about putting my thoughts on paper.

APPENDIX 1: PRACTICE WITH AUTHENTIC LANGUAGE (page 106)

1. success
2. better
3. painfully
4. miracle
5. you're
6. determination
7. most popular
8. cancerous
9. amputate
10. your
11. than
12. essential

Chapter 12

Possible answers:

1 PRESENT TIME TENSES AND SUBJECT-VERB AGREEMENT (page 88)

After most students graduate from college, they **find** nice jobs and begin earning money. However, few people take the time to investigate nontraditional opportunities that are available in nonprofit, public service, and government organizations. This seems to be a path that more recent graduates are currently exploring. Over the past decade, students **have had** the chance to choose from many types of employers and select the opportunity that **is** the most beneficial for each of them. Sometimes this may not be the job that pays the most money. Many times, the knowledge that a new graduate gains in a low-paying or nontraditional position **is** more valuable for his or her future. Spending two or three years in the Peace Corps or Teach America **helps** students learn about themselves and about the world around them. The monetary sacrifices a recent graduate **makes** will hopefully be rewarded in future positions. In addition to future job benefits, the friends and experiences that a person gains in less conventional positions are worth more than money. In other words, many of the sacrifices graduates **make** early in their careers will be fully rewarded later on. Volunteerism **is** another way to gain important job training and experience. New opportunities **come** from the most unexpected places, and many times volunteer work is that unexpected place. These kinds of opportunities present themselves throughout life, but the time to begin looking for them **is** now.

2 PAST TIME TENSES AND SUBJECT-VERB AGREEMENT (page 88)

I had always wanted to study and learn more about rain forests, and my opportunity finally **arrived** when a group of biology and botany students from all over the world organized a working holiday in Central America. I **signed up** right away.

The location that we were living and studying in **was** one of the best places in Central America to observe the wonders of the rain forest. On the first day, I saw the biodiversity that the rain forest **contained**. During the two months we **were** there, we saw plants and animals that I never **knew** existed. I think the diversity of life **was** incredible to even the most experienced students. Some of us had the rare opportunity to observe a plant that we **had never seen** before. Studying in this environment with amazing plants and animals was the best experience of my life.

When I **returned** from the rain forest, I was even more committed to preserving our environment. I **recommended** this kind of working holiday to all my fellow students. Even today I feel that this is an experience people from all fields should have in order to truly appreciate the world that we are living in and the delicate state it is in.

3 FUTURE TIME; TIME SHIFTS AND TENSE (page 89)

Why didn't I stop them? Why didn't I call the police? Why didn't I do anything at all? In horror, I turned back and **looked** at the bleeding man on the floor of the convenience store as the thieves were rushing out the door. I faced my cowardice and **felt** such agony. I experienced a lot of guilt for not acting. Shame rushed through my entire mind and body. Even though I **had** a cellular phone at the time, I never thought to call the police— all because I was scared. Until that moment, I always **believed** I was a tough person, someone who stood up for justice. However, at that instant, I saw a side of myself that I am still not proud of. Since that shameful day, I have often thought about that moment. In general, I know that fear **causes** people to behave in unexpected ways. Before that day, I thought I was above that. However, I was wrong. I **hope** that in the future, I will react differently. I **will try** to be more brave. Hopefully, I **will** never **experience** something that horrible again. However, if I do, I **am**

going to do the right thing. I now know that the shame I feel today is worse than the fear I **felt** on that day. Those few seconds **taught** me the importance of standing up for what I believe in rather than just talking about those beliefs. This is a lesson that I think **will change** my future behavior.

4 COUNT AND NONCOUNT NOUNS; ARTICLES AND OTHER DETERMINERS (page 90)

It was a cold night in the middle of winter, but the bright streetlights and yellow stars made the chilly, **35-degree** night seem a little warmer. It wasn't cold enough to snow, although a white covering of **snow** would have added to the winter scene. I was driving my bright red car, passing one **house** after another. I imagined the people behind each front **door** enjoying **a** family gathering and a nice dinner. All I felt was emptiness and absolute **loneliness**. My usual positive outlook was not able to melt the frosty feeling inside of me. I shook my head, trying to stop all the sad thoughts. Thinking too much wasn't going to help the situation anyway. I chose to give up the struggle going on inside my head and concentrate only on driving along the empty road. The **significance** of **the/that** moment was not clear to me at **the/that** time. All of that would become apparent in the next few **hours**.

5 PRONOUNS; DEMONSTRATIVE AND POSSESSIVE ADJECTIVES (page 90)

I learned an important lesson about friendship when I was fourteen years old. My family and **I** were living in a town that was out in the country. It was a small sleepy town whose school didn't offer many after-school activities other than playing basketball and just hanging out. I thought I was pretty good at both activities and did **them** whenever I could. I used to play basketball every day after school, after hanging out with my friends. Even though I played with **them** almost every day,

they didn't think I was good enough to join **their** competitive team. I noticed that all the competitive players in my town wore NBA basketball jerseys. I really wanted to join that team and thought that if I wore one, I would be allowed to join. My parents finally bought me two different team jerseys, and I was so happy with **these** jerseys. It was a very sad day for **me** when I wore a jersey and still wasn't asked to join the team. Later, it became clear that the team members were never interested in **me**. Not long after this, my family moved away, and I made new friends in **our** new town, but I'll never forget the lesson that I learned about friendship. True friends help **their** friends in all situations, not just when it's convenient.

6 MODALS; VERB FORMS, GERUNDS AND INFINITIVES (page 91)

Peer pressure **has been** a common problem for many high school students over the past several decades. Many teenagers feel they **cannot say** no to their friends because acceptance is very important at this time in their lives. Sometimes peer pressure can be positive and other times it can be negative. A lot of adolescents make their friends **begin** smoking, drinking, cutting school, and driving too fast. In contrast, a student **may decide** to study, play sports, and **join** clubs because of positive peer pressure. During the transition from junior high to high school, I saw the best student change to the worst student due to the bad influences of his peers. As a young adult, I now enjoy **thinking about** the many good influences in high school that helped me **to continue/continue** my education. Because I was fortunate to have positive role models during my teenage years, in my future career I plan **to help** teenagers who are facing many negative influences and are thinking about **giving in** to peer pressure. If a teenager has one positive role model, it **could mean** the difference between success and failure.

7 WORD FORMS (page 91)

It was a day like any other as Kellie and I started peddling away from school on our bike ride home. It was the **hottest** afternoon of the spring, and we **anticipated** spending it by Kellie's swimming pool. We had a lot of **boring** homework, but that could wait until we had worked on our tans for a few hours. After we had unlocked our bikes, Kellie rode away a little **faster** than I did. I followed her as she wove her way through the basketball and volleyball courts just as some of the teams were beginning to practice. As we approached a narrow passage between the tennis courts and the gym, we thought the way looked **clear**, and we turned the corner. To our **surprise**, the football players had just begun to make **their** way through the passage. This gave us barely enough room to maneuver ourselves and our bikes **past** them. The passage was **too** narrow for us to turn around, so we were forced to make our way **slowly** down the path with the football players coming toward us. Because there were no adults, some of these athletes grabbed our backpacks and made unkind remarks. At that moment I knew the true meaning of helplessness. The moment made Kellie and me feel **frightened**, but we sure learned to ride our bikes **quickly**!